AUSTRALIAN
ABORIGINAL RELIGION

FASCICLE TWO

INSTITUTE OF RELIGIOUS ICONOGRAPHY
STATE UNIVERSITY GRONINGEN

ICONOGRAPHY OF RELIGIONS

EDITED BY

Th. P. van Baaren, L. Leertouwer and H. Buning (*Secretary*)

SECTION V: AUSTRALIAN ABORIGINAL RELIGION

FASCICLE TWO

LEIDEN
E. J. BRILL
1974

AUSTRALIAN
ABORIGINAL RELIGION

BY

RONALD M. BERNDT

FASCICLE TWO
THE NORTH-EASTERN REGION AND NORTH AUSTRALIA

With 41 Plates and 2 folding Maps

LEIDEN
E. J. BRILL
1974

This Section consists of four Fascicles

ISBN 90 04 03726 8

PRINTED IN THE NETHERLANDS

CONTENTS

PREFACE

Fascicle Two continues the study of Australian Aboriginal religion.

In the last Fascicle (One), Aboriginal religion was discussed in general terms. The tremendous influence of the work of Émile Durkheim and A. R. Radcliffe-Brown on such studies was indicated, along with the potential influence of Claude Lévi-Strauss' more recent writings. In spite of these, a firm tone of empiricism has prevailed among contemporary Australian anthropologists concerned with this topic: they have focused on a consideration of Aboriginal religion in its socio-cultural setting, as something which is not separated from the mainstream of everyday affairs. Both analysis and statements about theoretical issues have mostly rested on that basis. Rather than interpreting the older work on Aboriginal religion in conjunction with what are often regarded as outmoded theories of religion, Australian anthropologists have preferred to look at it in the light of recent research, and from that standpoint to develop explanations along socio-cultural lines.

Central to an understanding of Aboriginal religion throughout the continent is the concept of the Dreaming. This emphasizes the idea of 'ever-present eternity', recognizing that the past has a bearing on the present and, indeed, on the future; and placing the responsibility of sacredness in the hands of living persons who are themselves seen as sharing a special essence or quality with all other living things, including the mythic beings. This concept of the Dreaming is reflected in totemism. The sphere of the sacred is relevant to all Aborigines, and is not confined to the specific area which is called the secret-sacred. It is in this respect that divergence from the earlier contributions, of Durkheim for example, is most obvious.

The aim of the present study is to delineate the patterns of Aboriginal religion. Aboriginal Australia was traditionally by no means uniform, socially, culturally or linguistically, even though basic themes such as the concept of the Dreaming were held in common. On one hand, then, my concern has been to establish an overall picture which could lead to more soundly framed generalizations about Aboriginal religion. On the other hand, I have attempted to spell out the wide range of variations which existed and continue to exist in many parts of Aboriginal Australia. Uniformity is apparent only when we stand back from the actual empirical situation.

Against this background, discussion moves from the general to the particular. Fascicle One pays special attention to south-eastern Australia. This area comes closest to what can be called a 'classic' type—mainly, perhaps, because of the earlier writers who were not anthropologists and whose work was extensively used by European armchair theorists on comparative religion. Of course, it was principally the publications of Sir Baldwin Spencer and F. J. Gillen that inspired Durkheim, as we shall see in Chapter Five (Fascicle Four); but these others contributed to no less a degree. The Aboriginal societies of south-eastern Australia are no longer in existence, and most of the cultural knowledge has disappeared.

In this Fascicle (Two), we turn to a further consideration of a particular area. In some respects this is linked to the last (in so far as the *bora* complex is concerned), but it also has (in the north-east: Cape York Peninsula) strong affiliations with the religious patterns of North Australia. These too are treated here, in part, but are continued into Fascicle Three.

In the preparation of this material, the iconography of Aboriginal religion emerges within its socio-cultural context—as objects and things used, and not as objects and things separated from their own particular settings. Nevertheless each Chapter, with its regional concentration, includes a specific section on this topic. Each regional outline is followed by a bibliography to provide convenient access to sources. This has been considered necessary because in each Chapter references are made to the work of many writers, and the reader can see directly at a glance the range of literature relevant to the area being considered. Also, since the four fascicles which make up the total span of this study of Australian Aboriginal religion are being published separately, it would not be practical or convenient to have all the bibliographies arranged as an entity at the end of Fascicle Four. As mentioned, this Fascicle also deals with the first part of the North Australian material. It is unfortunate that it must be broken, to continue into Fascicle Three: but for publishing reasons this has proved essential. The Bibliography to that Chapter (Four) is to be found in Fascicle Three.

Department of Anthropology,   Ronald M. BERNDT
University of Western Australia

CHAPTER THREE

THE NORTH-EASTERN REGION

Anthropological material on Aboriginal religion in Queensland is scattered and to some extent limited. Among earlier writers, Roth (publishing between 1897 and 1910) provides a great deal of data. So does R. H. Mathews (between 1896-1908), among others. (See Craig 1967; 1970). It has not been possible to cover all of this, even in summary, and the references are a small selection from a very large number available. Nevertheless, some dominant trends are apparent.

As has been mentioned, Dieri culture shows signs of interaction with people from the south-western corner of Queensland. On the other hand, the Aurukun people on Cape York (McCarthy 1964) were probably influenced by eastern Arnhem Landers. Additionally, there were both general and more specific influences on Cape York culture from Papua and the Torres Strait Islands (see Haddon 1901-35; McConnel 1936: 452; etc.).

1. THE DORA-MOLONGA COMPLEX

The religious patterns relevant to New South Wales (see Chapter 2) extended into south-eastern Queensland. Howitt (1904: 595-99) writes of rituals being focused on the triennial harvest of *bunya* tree fruit. The Turrbal, occupying territory on the Brisbane River, held the *kurbin-aii* initiation rites when the *bunya-bunya* fruit were ripe and the sea mullet came in. Around the ritual ground, trees were cut with figures, and when the bullroarers were swung it was said that native doctors swallowed the novices. There were food tabus, ritualized conflict, and men decorated for dancing.

The *dora* (in the vicinity of Maryborough, Howitt *ibid.*: 599-607) differed from the New South Wales *bora*: no magic or native doctors were referred to, and proceedings were run by older men. The decision to hold such a ritual rested on the report of an elder that he had seen in a vision an eaglehawk, regarded as a fighting bird. The *dora* ground was encircled by a mound of earth and logs, with a track leading into the scrub, where a space was cleared and a platform constructed. Women with firesticks stood bunched tightly together on top of the mound and, before leaving, threw these into the circle. Novices accompanied by guardians were protected from simulated attacks, and the crux of the initiation rite was the bestowal of new names on the novices. These names enabled them 'to catch fish or animals, or to do something relating to hunting'. At this time, novices were given weapons by their guardians and were instructed in fighting. In fact, fighting was a cultural focus; and there was conventionalized combat, followed by the swinging of bullroarers. Howitt (*ibid.*: 498-500) speaks of a being named Birral (equated with Baiami), 'who lived in an island further north to which place he directs their ghosts after death'. Farther north again, Howitt says, a being named Kohin was associated with a special object called *tikovina* (*ibid.*: fig. 28, 499), a 'war-charm' usually worn round the neck. Roth (1909: 166-85) provides further examples of initiation rituals.

Among the Koko-yimidir, of 'Yir-Yoront type' (see below), a circular initiation ground (*boral*) was made, with a U-shaped trench near its centre. On one side a low bush fence was constructed, and there novices slept with their guardians. Dances dramatizing the actions of natural species were held on this ground, watched by novices squatting in the trench. Some were strikingly similar to those of Central Australia. In one, a beeswax model of a fish was used. Others were obviously of increase intent. In the final performance of the series, the trench was obliterated by dancing feet. Later, an emblem representing honey in a hollow tree was placed in the ground where the trench had been, rendering the site tabu. The novices were red-ochred, and returned to the main camp. There were also a number of subsidiary rites, one involving bullroarers, and presentation of one of these to a novice. This object was called 'snake', and was believed to have power to kill snakes as well as people. A snake dance followed, when the novices were shown a large carpet snake fixed to a tree. The presence of a trench with novices placed within it, along with the snake association, has parallels with sacred *kunapipi* ritual. (See Chapter Four.)

In Roth's other examples, there are variations on this theme. Some involved piercing of the nasal septum; others, cicatrization. In one initiation ritual at Princess Charlotte Bay, the sacred ground was constructed with a short entrance way leading to where decorated postulants performed dances relating to natural species. Many of these had to do with food restrictions for novices, and the lifting of such tabus. The Koko-warra ritual, within the same area, had six initiatory stages. In one, masked dancers (see below) called Amboiba buffeted the novices. Roth (1897: 120-25) also describes the *molonga* ritual, which supposedly referred to an unpredictable spirit. A hut divided the dancing ground, one side being associated with men and the other with women. Dancers wore conical headdresses. In the final part, Molonga himself appeared and, later, a dancer entered holding a flat piece of wood, covered with a feather-down design representing female genitals. Roth also describes (*ibid.*: 170-80), for the Boulia district, both circumcision and subincision rites which did not differ radically from those in Central and Northern Territory areas, and female initiation (defloration and introcision: see also R. and C. Berndt 1964/68: 150-5).

One difficulty with most of this earlier material is that it provides only a limited insight into ritual patterning, without integrating this with mythic and other meanings. The rites are not seen in their broader religious perspective. For example, while the U-shaped trench conforms to Kunapipi pattern, not enough evidence is available to allow us to make a meaningful connection. The mythic and social significance of the *molonga* is missing, although Elkin (1964: 300-1) points out that it was found over a wide area—from the Worgaia, at the head of the Georgina, to the Dieri of Lake Eyre, and on to the Great Australian Bight (see Howitt *ibid.*: 416, fig. 23).

2. Cape York Peninsula

The work of Ursula McConnel, Lauriston Sharp and D. Thomson in the 1930's is more relevant to this discussion. Further research has been done since then, but much of the results of this is still unpublished: see Craig (1967; 1970). McConnel concentrated on the Wik-Munkan (Wik-Mungkan) and adjacent tribes of Cape York Peninsula. These had patrilineal territorially-focused clans, each with a number of 'totems', some reflecting economic interests, others possessing negative social interests. Not all of these 'totems' were natural species; many were items and objects of everyday use. Personal names were derived from these, and there was an intimate bond between a person and his clan totem (*pulwaiya*). Each had its sacred place of origin (McConnel 1930: 181-203), its *auwa*. (This was the *kol'a* of the Koko Ya'o: see Thomson 1933: 469.) Near its waters lived the *pulwaiya*, and into this site spirits of the dead were believed to go. During rites at an *auwa* to ensure a plentiful supply of that particular *pulwaiya* in its 'natural', manifest form, appeals were made to these spirits. Rituals differed from one *auwa* to another, but it was to the spirits of the dead, who presumably had become *pulwaiya*, that invocations were called; and these *pulwaiya* had associated myths. Moreover, all *auwa* had spirit children connected with them. For example, at male and female *auwa* sites of the ghost clan, were child-*auwa* of both sexes. Women who desired to have children would participate in the relevant rites. (See also McConnel 1957:142-49.) On the bestowal of the boy's totemic name, he came under the protection of the *pulwaiya* 'and [acquired] the hunting rights and privileges of his father's clan' (McConnel 1934: 318). McConnel emphasized the religious significance of clan ancestors, and of the myths and rituals concerning food supplies: each clan looked to a common ancestor (the *pulwaiya*). Food supplies were a special focus. For example, a clan in charge of a particular species always engaged in a ritualistic 'taking' of the relevant food before members of other clans were permitted to tap that resource.

The framework of initiation ritual was held in common with many other groups. A youth was separated from the main camp, in the face of active or passive protests from women, and subjected to strict speech and food tabus which were lifted ritually only at its conclusion, with the participation of women. The swinging of a bullroarer signified social recognition of manhood; but it was also swung during female puberty rites for 'girls-who-have-reached-maturity'. The significance of women in regard to male ritual found mythical expression in a Wik-Munkan belief connected with the Bonefish (boney bream) cult: the bullroarer was said to have been found by a mature girl, who hid it in a bloodwood tree for men to swing (McConnel 1935: 67-71, plate I,A). In another myth, the same girl (or girls) said, in reference to this object, 'It belongs to us women really, we have found it! But no matter! We leave it for the men! It is they who will always use it!' (*ibid.*: 68-9; 1957: 119-24). In the relevant rite, the 'girl' was depicted swinging a bullroarer: this was part of initiation, and there are other similar examples. In another rite, an actor representing Bonefish emerged from a bloodwood tree holding his large penis, accompanied by his 'wife'; symbolically, this meant that the 'husband's' penis was fanned into creative activity to ensure a plentiful supply of boney bream (*ibid.* 1957: 41). Bullroarers were of four varieties, representing *i* a young girl at puberty; *ii* a more mature girl; *iii* and *iv* a husband and wife—one symbolizing a penis, the other a fully-grown woman. Regarding the last, two actors representing husband and 'wife' acted out various ritual scenes: in one, the 'woman' lay down and had a wax image of a baby placed on 'her' belly. McConnel, describing this rite, says that it demonstrated the continuity of life through the sexual act and birth, and the bullroarers 'reflect the various stages in the development of sex-relationship' (*ibid.*: 1935: 70; 1957: 131-3). Other examples emphasize the sexual nature of these objects.

Thomson (1933: 461-89), for the Koko Ya'o, also discusses initiation rites. Two series were involved, inspired by the culture hero I'wai. In both, the secret-sacred *ko'ol* screen was an important focus—behind it sacred objects were prepared and stored, and dances were held. Both series included a large number of dances, some of the actors representing mythic beings wearing masks. One dramatized the myth of the Rainbow Snake swallowing a novice.

Returning to the *pulwaiya*, McConnel notes (1936: Part I, 456-77; Part II, 69-105) that each *pulwaiya*-cult was controlled by members of a relevant clan but the actual rites performed at a particular site were believed to bestow benefits upon all members of the society, and that the *pulwaiya* was really a cult hero. The more socially significant a particular *pulwaiya*, the more specialized its cult, mythology and ritual, graded in 'a kind of hierarchy' according to the relative importance of the *pulwaiya*. Myths concerning *pulwaiya* tell of the transformation of these totemic beings and the inauguration of their ritual. This involved drama, dance and song which were gradually revealed to initiates, during or after initiation. McConnel gives examples, drawing attention to the transformation of the *pulwaiya* into their totemic forms: the rites re-enacted their activities, and some of them were performed in the main camp, others in secret. The mythic heroes of tribes north of the Wik-Munkan, says McConnel, wandered 'more restlessly' and were 'more humanly' active than the Wik-Munkan heroes: the latter were spatially restricted around their *auwa* (sites, or 'story places'), as the others were not. McConnel recorded a large number of myths (1936: 69-105; 1935: 66-93; 1931: 9-25; 1957), not summarized here. In the case of the Shiveri (Seagull) and Nyunggu (Torres Strait Pigeon) myth, for example, which has linkages with Torres Strait Islands and the Papuan mainland, McConnel takes up Thomson (1934a: 226-9) on a number of points of interpretation. Another myth, of the Rainbow (see McConnel 1930: 347-9), is also relevant to Koko Ya'o initiation, and there are other points of comparison with ritual and myth elsewhere in Aboriginal Australia. For instance, the Wik-Munkan equated blood used in initiation, with the menstrual flow (McConnel 1936: 85-6). Thomson (1934a: 227-9) provides a glimpse of the Thungundji Sivirri and Ernyongo (Shiveri and Nyunggu) initiation rite, which took place on a sacred ground with an enclosure, where masked figures played an important part in the drama, to the beating of drums.

For the Wik-Munkan, the two ends of the life-cycle revolved round the *auwa*. After a death (McConnel 1937: 346-64), mourning dances were held while the corpse was still in the camp, before its cremation, and the songs sung related to the Ghost clan myth, telling of the tragic end of an ancestral husband and wife. The deceased's spirit was identified with the *auwa*, and believed to be transformed into the relevant totem species. According to McConnel (1937: 361), the spirits of the dead of a particular clan assumed the clan totem form 'in order to participate in the perpetuation of the species, by mating' and reproducing: they performed the same function as the *pulwaiya*. Thomson (1933: 493-505), however, drew a distinction between two kinds of totem, mainly in regard to the Koko Ya'o. There, the Wik-Munkan *pulwaiya* was the *pola*, the patrilineal cult totem; the other was a personal 'totem' (called the *ngartjimo ngorntadji*), which was not inherited at birth but came from the mother's moiety or clan 'by augury commencing soon after birth and culminating in the removal of an upper central incisor tooth' (*ibid.*: 493). Every person thus had two spirits at birth: one left and went to the mother's country at the closure of the frontal suture, but was enticed back by means of ritual; the other remained with a person until death, when it became a ghost. Tooth evulsion itself was not ritualized; but a member of a novice's matri-moiety (usually his elder sister's son) would give him a totem name from his own patri-clan: and this was manifested as the boy's personal totem, connected with his mother's country, linking with the one which had left him or had returned to him; on death this link was continued. The Koko Ya'o situation is not as clear-cut as the Wik-Munkan.

The Yir-Yoront near the Mitchell River also had patrilineal clans connected with particular totems. These were actually clan ancestors 'who lived at the beginning of time and continue their existence as spirits' for the benefit of the clan, were focused on sites, and were concerned with natural resources (Sharp 1934b: 19-42). Myths and rituals were associated with them, as with those in the Wik-Munkan area. One aim of the rituals was to introduce youths to their ancestral heritage; another was the increase of natural species, etc. Sharp says (1934b: 22) that a spirit child was not linked with a person's ancestors. However, the evidence he provides suggests otherwise. Each clan had a water spirit centre where a particular male or female ancestor resided, sending out spirit children as the occasion demanded. These spirits were transformed into various natural species who, as agents, would enter a mother after having been seen or found by her (Sharp 1934b: 23-4). The spirit child linked the unborn infant with the clan site, even though the agent (that into which it had been transformed) was not significant totemically. The ritual patterning was somewhat complex. The Yir-Yoront had various group rituals, some relating to increase, others to 'historical' incidents, to the Rainbow Snake, to mortuary occasions, and to compulsory initiation. In the secret parts of such rites, a series of mythic episodes was shown to novices. However, tooth evulsion and cicatrization were not ritualized and there was no circumcision, although bullroarers were used. Individual increase rites were performed at mythic 'holes' (the Wik-Munkan *auwa*).

Sharp's studies leave many gaps, but his survey of totemism in north-east Australia (1939: 254-75, 439-61) does bring together, in summary form, material from a hundred-odd tribes. For the 'Yir-Yoront type', in which the Wik-Munkan are included, he gives the following picture. Female initiation was lacking, and in male initiation blood played no part. All initiation rites had to do with the representation of totems and ancestral events. Throughout the area designated by this 'type' (that is, on the western side of Cape York), spirit children and conception appeared in varied froms. It was customary for a pre-natal spirit child to be found and transferred by a husband to his wife through the medium of food: or it could appear as an agent (as noted above). In some parts of the area, the spirit child was believed to have existed from mythical times. Normally, there was a connection between the country of the prospective father and the place where the spirit child was 'found'. Sharp says there was little information on the fate of the pre-existent 'totemic' personal spirit at death. There were several variations. He reports the Wik-Munkan belief that the spirit returned to its *auwa*, but does not distinguish between differing kinds of spirit (as Thomson did). Nor is it clear what a 'totemic personal spirit' was, in this context.

THE ICONOGRAPHIC CONTEXT

The *dora-molonga* complex duplicates, to some extent, the south-eastern Australian versions combined with the Lake Eyre Basin (Dieri type). Bullroarers were in evidence in all initiation ritual. In some areas there were human figures, cut out on trees, and beeswax models as among the Koko-yimidir. The *molonga*, especially, included elaborate body painting, and a distinctive conical headdress resembling those used in the *kunapipi* of the north. Roth (1897: Plate XVI) provides examples in which dancers held various sticks and weapons.

In northern Queensland, exemplified by the Wik-Munkan and Yir-Yoront, bullroarers were used in dramatic re-enactments of the clan totem (*pulwaiya*, or its equivalent), during or after initiation. Among the Wik-Munkan these had a special symbolic significance relevant to 'the continuity of life', paralleling Northern Territory examples. It is probable that, in looking at the differing symbolism of bullroarers, a major distinction could be drawn between the northern 'life-charged' varieties, and those less directly related to fertility as in the *bora*, *dora* and probably Dieri examples. But in all cases, the sound of the bullroarer was the voice of a mythic being.

Each *pulwaiya* had its own distinctive set of decorations and ritual paraphernalia. The sacred objects kept behind the *ko'ol* screen of the Koko Ya'o were mostly masks. Roth (1909: Plates L, LI, LIII) gives some examples, and so does Thomson (1933) for the I'wai rituals. These masks, in the shape of a crocodile head (see McCarthy 1957: 126A), were used along with drums. Movable masks, however, were almost certainly introduced from Papua. At the same time, the equivalent of a mask, where the faces of ritual actors were covered in feather-down and ochred designs, was common throughout Aboriginal Australia.

In summary and on a broader canvas, influences from the New South Wales initiatory complex are apparent in the *dora*, except that magic was excluded and conventional fighting and wrestling competitions were the norm. Especially significant was the bestowal of 'power-giving' names on novices to aid them in hunting. And a supernatural being was identified with Baiami. On the north-western side of the region, the *molonga* complex came down into the Dieri area, probably owing its origin (at least in part) to the western New South Wales *bora*. It could be seen, from the evidence available, as a kind of revitalization of the *bora* but in a different guise, the *bora* itself being changed as it was pushed farther inland and away from the main waterways by increasing alien settlement pressures.

In the northern sector, around the Cape York Peninsula area, the Wik-Munkan-Yir-Yoront formed a religious bloc distinct from the southern region. Within it, religious variations were obvious. So were social organizational totemic patterns (see Sharp 1939, who distinguished five major ones). But the overview as far as religious belief and action are concerned shows clan sites associated with totemic spirit beings sometimes identified as ancestors, and these served as reservoirs of unborn spirit children. Increase rites focused on these sites have close parallels in the Central regions of Australia—for example, in the Desert complex. (See Chapter Five.) Over and above localized increase rites were large mytho-ritual constellations involving initiation and 'cult hero' ceremonies (rituals), which were mostly re-enactments of myths. Initiation rites involved bullroarers; and beliefs surrounding them, and the ritual expressions themselves, provide a pattern that is typically 'northern' (for instance, of Arnhem Land type). Concentration on fertility, both human and animal, on the ritual and mythic significance of females, and on the continuity of social living through sexual activity, birth and re-birth—all of these emphasize the comparison which can be made here. Also within this picture is the Rainbow Snake—an element which, although it has been reported very widely indeed throughout Aboriginal Australia, could be an indication of linkage with the north-west (Arnhem Land) fertility cults.

BIBLIOGRAPHY

Berndt, R. M. and C. H. 1964/68. *The World of the First Australians*: Ure Smith, Sydney.

Craig, B. F. (Compiler). 1967. *Cape York*: Bibliography Series, No. 2, Occasional Papers in Aboriginal Studies No. 9. Australian Institute of Aboriginal Studies, Canberra.

Craig, B. F. (Compiler). 1970. *North-West-Central Queensland. An Annotated Bibliography*: Bibliography Series, No. 6, Australian Aboriginal Studies No. 41, Australian Institute of Aboriginal Studies, Canberra.

Elkin, A. P. 1938/1964. *The Australian Aborigines*: Angus and Robertson, Sydney.

Haddon, A. C. 1901-35. In *Cambridge Anthropological Expedition to Torres Strait. Reports*: Cambridge University Press, Cambridge.

Howitt, A. W. 1904. *The Native Tribes of South-East Australia*: Macmillan, London.

McCarthy, F. D. 1957. *Australia's Aborigines, Their Life and Culture*. Colorgravure Publications, Melbourne.

McCarthy, F. D. 1964. The Dancers of Aurukun, *Australian Natural History*, Vol. 14, No. 9.

McConnel, U. 1930a. The Wik-Munkan Tribe. Part II, Totemism, *Oceania*, Vol. I, No. 2.

McConnel, U. 1930b. The Rainbow-Serpent in North Queensland, *Oceania*, Vol. I, No. 3.

McConnel, U. 1931. A Moon Legend from the Bloomfield River, North Queensland, *Oceania*, Vol. II, No. 1.

McConnel, U. 1934. The Wik-Munkan and Allied Tribes of Cape York Peninsula, North Queensland. Part III. Kinship and Marriage, *Oceania*, Vol. IV, No. 3.

McConnel, U. 1935. Myths of the Wikmunkan and Wiknatara tribes, *Oceania*, Vol. VI, No. 1.

McConnel, U. 1936. Totemic Hero-Cults in Cape York Peninsula, North Queensland, Parts I and II, *Oceania*, Vol. VI, No. 4; Vol. VII, No. 1.

McConnel, U. 1937. Mourning Ritual Among the Tribes of Cape York Peninsula, *Oceania*, Vol. VII, No. 3.

McConnel, U. 1957. *Myths of the Mungkan*: Melbourne University Press, Melbourne.

Roth, W. E. 1897. *Ethnological Studies among the North-west-Central Queensland Aborigines*: Government Printer, Brisbane/London.

Roth, W. E. 1909. North Queensland Ethnography, No. 12. On Certain Initiation Ceremonies, *Records of the Australian Museum*, Vol. VII, No. 3.

Sharp, R. L. 1934a. The Social Organization of the Yir-Yoront Tribe, Cape York Peninsula, *Oceania*, Vol. IV, No. 4.

Sharp, R. L. 1934b. Ritual Life and Economics of the Yir-Yoront of Cape York Peninsula, *Oceania*, Vol. V, No. 1.

Sharp, R. L. 1939. Tribes and Totemism in North-East Australia, *Oceania*, Vol. IX, Nos. 3 and 4.

Thomson, D. F. 1933. The Hero Cult, Initiation and Totemism on Cape York, *Journal of the Royal Anthropological Institute*, Vol. LXIII.

Thomson, D. F. 1934a. Notes on a Hero Cult from the Gulf of Carpentaria, North Queensland, *Journal of the Royal Anthropological Institute*, Vol. LXIV.

Thomson, D. F. 1934b. The Dugong Hunters of Cape York, *Journal of the Royal Anthropological Institute*, Vol. LXIV.

CHAPTER FOUR

NORTH AUSTRALIA

The region considered here is spatially extensive and culturally complex. Roughly, it includes the upper northern sector of the Northern Territory as far south as the upper reaches of the Victoria River around Wave Hill, the Barkly Tableland, and the Kimberley districts of Western Australia. Modern anthropological material is sparse for some of these areas, especially for the Barkly Tableland, which is mentioned only incidentally. Again, it is necessary to be selective. Rather than spreading the discussion too thinly, we shall focus on two inter-connected spheres. The first is the interplay between religion and the life cycle; the second, the fertility cults.

RELIGION AND THE LIFE CYCLE

i. *Birth*

The theme referred to in the *Introduction* (Chapter One) underlined the belief that contemporary Aboriginal man was linked to the Dreaming, to the creative era, and contained within himself part of the essence of the mythic beings. In some areas, contemporary Aborigines saw themselves as living representatives of such beings. This concept, however, is not obviously expressed in Northern Australia, although it is presumably just as significant. In Warner's view (1937/58: 125-37), a 'Murngin' boy gradually enhanced his career through involvement in sacred activities, initiatory grades; but girls remained in the 'profane' camp with no such progression. However, conception and birth provide indicators of spiritual affinity, since in eastern Arnhem Land the spirits of unborn children are believed to reside in 'totem clan wells' along with totemic species (*ibid.*: 68). Also, a father's dream identifies a pre-natal spirit child, which is believed to enter its prospective mother at quickening. The well from which it came, located in the father's territory, is of Dreaming significance and therefore sacred. Warner contended that a child enters a profane world and that all his future activities are focused on accumulating sacredness in ritually defined ways. The evidence suggests, rather, that he enters that world possessing already an innate sacredness. In 'Murngin' belief, the bones of both male and female children are likened to secret-sacred *rangga* emblems, symbolizing the poles originally removed from the Djanggawul sisters (R. Berndt 1952: 7). The unborn child is associated with a particular natural species, and bears a direct relationship to the great *wongar* (Dreaming) spirits (R. and C. Berndt 1964/68: 183). It is true that males are expected, in fact obliged, to participate in ritual to enhance their sacredness. But one implication of the material is that for females this sacred basis is enough: that their sacredness requires no such enhancement.

On Groote Eylandt (Turner 1970), pre-natal spirits come from the clan territory of the prospective fathers and are (or were until quite recently) 'sung' into mothers shortly before birth. The songs concern tracks of mythic beings associated with the particular part of the country relevant to the spirit child, and in this way the child's name (that is, with mythic linkage) is chosen. A spirit child is called *alawudawara*, a term which classes it with mythic beings, the Dreaming, and a deceased person's spirit, among other things. The word can be translated as 'part of the supernatural'. What is revealing in this connection, as Turner points out, is that the child spirit *is* of the supernatural, not something that has simply come into a special relationship with it and is therefore subject to tabus until normalized.

In north-eastern and western Arnhem Land, a spirit-child animator makes itself known to its potential father while he is out hunting or fishing, and appears in conjunction with a natural species but is not actually identified with it—not 'totemically' identified, in the sense of ritual or other commitments in later life. In western Arnhem Land there are also said to be repositories of spirit children at particular sites (R. and C. Berndt 1951: 83). Among the Gunwinggu, however, the place of birth or 'conception' (quickening) is not significant in religious affairs (R. and C. Berndt 1970: 105). In spite of this, the spiritual tie between father and child is important (R. Berndt 1966: 9-13). The creature which serves as the agent or vehicle is *gaingen*, 'flesh-concerning', and represents the material aspect, having no 'totemic' or ritual connotation. But the spirit-animator comes from or is part of the sacred, even though this is apparently diffused. In any case, the mythic *ubar* (ritual) Mother gave birth to the first children (people). Among the Maung, a coastal people of the same area, a spirit child is connected with a *djang* spirit (R. and C. Berndt 1970: 18-27) and/or with a creature not necessarily of mythic origin. *Djang* are sacred and linkage with them makes the spirit itself sacred. The word Yarlial refers to a place where a potential father 'finds' a pre-natal spirit child. The site is usually a swamp or stretch of water. He gives his wife a baler shell of clear water: the spirit is in this, and passes into her as she drinks. It is said that these spirit children come from a special island situated north of the Goulburn islands: visible by night, by day it sinks into the sea. Among both Gunwinggu and Maung, pregnant women used to wear a small dillybag, believed to hold part of the child's spirit (R. and C. Berndt 1951: 82). The symbolism of the dillybag-as-a-uterus appears in mythic accounts all along the Arnhem Land coast. Spencer (1914: 328-30) provides a similar example for the Kakadu (Gagadju), who originally lived in the Oenpelli area.

Spencer (*ibid.*: 263-74) also notes several examples which link pre-natal spirit children with mythic beings. The Mungarai (Mangarei) belief was that, when mythic beings shook themselves, spirit children in the totemic shape of the character concerned would fall to the ground: these served as 'storehouses' for future generations of pregnant women. There are many variations on this theme—for the Roper River tribes and those to the south-west of southern Arnhem Land, as for the Wadaman and Mudbara. For the Kakadu, Spencer (*ibid.*: 274) remarks 'that the child within the woman is the actual representative of one special individual amongst the old ancestors'.

Spirit children (*pitapitui*) among the Tiwi (of Bathurst and Melville Islands) are associated with particular sites in *imunga* matrilineal clan territories. They are found in dreams by potential fathers, who say they appear in human form while women say they resemble birds (Goodale 1959*b*: 89, 94-5). Mountford (1958: 146-50) underlines a relationship between the *pitapitui* and Purukupali, a mythic being who was responsible for obtaining *pitapitui* for his two creative sisters. M. Brandl (1971) says that, since a woman during childbirth is in a *pukumani* (dangerous, tabu-ed) state, this probably indicates that the newly born child is 'sacred equals dangerous'—because it has come from the spirit world.

To Port Keats Aborigines (primarily the Murinbata, within the so-called 'Brinken bloc'), every person has a spirit which existed prior to his birth and will continue after death (Falkenberg 1962: 238-58). This reveals itself as either *ngarit'ngarit* (made by Nugemain, a mythic being) or *kura'manganat* (made by Kun'manggur, the Rainbow). (See also Stanner 1936: 193-6.) Without our considering the problem of such dual origin, pre-natal spirit children are found in much the same way as in other areas—but in this case, not through dreams. They are said to reveal themselves during unusual circumstances, are associated with particular tracts of country, and must be 'found' by certain relatives who are usually members of the potential father's clan. Stanner (1933: 27-8) reports that, among the Nangiomeri, spirit children (*mambir*) enter a woman through food while bathing. *Mambir*, he says, 'originally came out of a rock from which a spring gushed in dream-times, and now are to be found in all permanent water'. But he adds (1959-61: 251-2, 253-4), for the Murinbata, that it seems each person's private 'totem' (*mir*) links a spirit child with some non-human entity made by the ancestors, and that this is identified by an incident associated with a child's conception: the *ngarit'ngarit* (spirit child) uses this incident to draw a husband's attention to the fact that his wife has conceived. The *mir* (or 'soul') is the agent of the spirit child.

Meggitt (1962: 65-7, 272-3, 277) speaks of the Walbiri (Wailbri) belief in *guruwari* spirit-entities, or centres 'at which dreamtime beings have deposited part of their spiritual or dreaming-essence'. As in the Mungarai example, they did this by shaking their ritual feather-down decorations—these feathers were dislodged, and falling to the ground became various natural features, species, etc., which also became *guruwari*. *Guruwari*, according to Meggitt, are impersonal and causally-effective entities. Every Walbiri has a conception-dreaming. The *guruwari* enters a pregnant woman and animates the foetus: its identity is dependent on where the woman camped—that is, at which Dreaming site—and where she first realized her pregnancy. Fortuitous as this circumstance might appear to be, it means that a direct association is established between the spirit (as animator) of a child and, through the *guruwari* as an intermediary, the great mythic beings.

Kaberry (1939:31, 41-5, 194-5) speaks of special pools at which a spirit child is found by a prospective father. However, these children or *djinganarany* are not ancestral, but are said to have been put in such places by Kaleru the Rainbow Snake, who is Dreaming, *ngarungani* (or *ngaranggani*). The spirit child is temporarily incarnated in a natural species. Beliefs in this respect vary throughout the east and south Kimberleys. Quite common is the view that such a spirit enters a pregnant woman through food, making its presence known through vomiting. Simultaneously, her husband dreams of some natural species which he associates with his wife's experience: it is that food or species which becomes the child's *djering*, conception totem. Reference is also made, in this context, to the spirit of a dead person being reborn. Kaberry emphasizes the link between a child and his or her spiritual background: as a spirit, he/she was 'created long ago by one of the totemic ancestors' and is, on birth, human. (See also Kaberry 1936: 392-400.) Kaberry, like Elkin (1933), mentions the re-touching of the Wondjina-head cave paintings (Kimberleys, Western Australia), believed to result in 'the going forth of spirit-children to be found by fathers and incarnated through their wives'.

For the Walmadjeri-Gugadja (Balgo area; R. Berndt 1971), mythic beings are mediated through their contemporary representatives, who take human shape through conception and birth. Some creature or plant, when killed or eaten, 'turns into' or is manifested through or becomes a living, contemporary human being. The *djarin* (Kaberry's *djering*) is identified with the *waldjiri*, which is a local group mythic indicator, or 'cult totem'. In areas farther north and north-west, these two labels are distinguished. In the Walmadjeri-Gugadja region a direct linkage is recognized between spirit child, *djarin*, *djugur* (Dreaming) and myth-ritual expression.

The evidence, in general, suggests a fairly intimate association between the pre-natal spirit and man on one hand, and the Dreaming beings on the other. As Stanner (1959-61: 120-1) puts it, 'Life already *was* in the Dreaming' and 'the bearers of non-corporeal life are child-spirits ...' They are the vehicle through which life *per se* is transferred from the Dreaming, from the mythic beings themselves, to human beings: and this is essentially a sacred transference, providing a basis for what takes place later in life. The equation is that life equals sacredness; and, if we wanted to be pedantic, we could say that there is a distinction between *natural* sacredness (that which is directly emergent from the Dreaming) and that which is invoked or simulated (that is, through ritual action). In saying this, we need not detract from that essential core of sacredness possessed by all Aborigines. There are other important themes in this context which we will not explore here. One is water: the Rainbow is a symbol of this and is widely associated with spirit children. The other is land: the actual site relevant to the material vehicle—as natural species etc.—of the spirit child, and in turn directly relevant to particular mythic beings and to group membership through patri-descent. See also Ashley-Montagu (1937) and Petri (1968: 274-76).

ii. *Initiation*

Coming from the sacred, Aboriginal man is exposed to a mundane world, the everyday life of the camp and its economic activities. But the sacred element is not dissipated, and socialization processes bring increasing involvement in religious ritual—whether the person concerned is male or female.

Initiation for boys is an introduction, or rather a *re*-introduction, to the sacred. The age at which the process formally begins varies. In eastern Arnhem Land, for instance, a boy is normally circumcised at between 6 and 8 years old.

Elkin says (1938/64: 198) that initiation rituals are patterned on 'the greatest transition rite of all, namely, death; indeed, it is really a pre-enactment of death and of the rising which it is desired should follow death'. R. and C. Berndt (1964/68: 136-39 *et seq.*) emphasize this and the emergence of the novice as a person who has now entered the sphere of social adulthood; even if he is still only on its fringes, he has achieved a new status. The physical ordeals that he undergoes during this period, where these are appropriate, mark his acceptance of the discipline entailed in his training, although symbolically these rites have other significance. Generally, however, initiation is *not* so much a ritual death or a ritual rebirth. The focus is on life, on sacredness, and on a greater identification with the mythic beings. It is not so much a 'rising' as a re-emergence, a ratification of what was there before, is there now, and must be developed.

For girls, on the other hand, the equivalent of initiation usually takes the form of puberty rites; but even the most elaborate of these are not so formalized nor so prolonged (R. and

C. Berndt 1964/68: 150-5). Their 'sacredness', we might say, does not need constant ratification, since they have essential life-giving properties within themselves—as pro-creators. With this in mind, it is probable that physiological maternity is recognized more generally than physiological paternity. Certainly, in the ideology of male descent through-out Australia spiritual elements are usually stressed (see R. Berndt 1970b: 1063-4).

The literature on initiation is especially extensive, and what will be discussed here will be very much in summary.

In north-eastern Arnhem Land, male initiation sequences are set in the context of four major ritual cycles—the *djunggawon*, *kunapipi*, *ngurlmag* and the *dua* and *jiridja* (yiridja) moiety *nara*. All include both novices and postulants, but only the *djunggawon* relates to circumcision: the others will therefore be noted later. However, the first three are sub-stantiated by the great Wawalag myth.

This myth is reported in several published accounts, starting with Warner (1937/58: 250-9), and followed by R. Berndt (1951a: 19-32), R. and C. Berndt (1964/68: 212-3), Lévi-Strauss (1962: 120-8) and C. Berndt (1970: 1306-26). Briefly, two sisters came northward to the coast from their home in the so-called Wawalag country, somewhere in the direction of the Roper River. They did not create plants, birds and animals, or places, but were responsible for naming many of them. The last site where they camped on their journey was the sacred waterhole of Muruwul, or Miraraminar. But within this lay hidden the great Rock Python, Julunggul (Yulunggul), sometimes identified with the Rainbow Snake. The two sisters tried to cook various creatures and plants they had collected on the way: but all of these got up from the coals and ran into the waterhole: in doing so they became sacred (*mareiin*) or 'totemic'—or, their sacredness became evident. The elder sister was pregnant, and gave birth to a child: afterbirth blood fell into the waterhole. (Warner notes menstrual blood; C. Berndt, either afterbirth blood from the elder sister or menstrual blood from the younger, or both.) Julunggul emerged in a great storm, with thunder and lightning. The Wawalag tried various ruses to restrain him, but he swallowed them, regurgitated them, and swallowed them again. While this was happening, the first rains of the north-west monsoon were falling and beginning to flood the land. In the final sequence, Julunggul (or a pair of Julunggul, as husband and wife) stood erect and spoke with other Rock Pythons in other parts of eastern Arnhem Land. He admitted having swallowed the Wawalag, and at the same time uttered a loud noise which is now the sound of the bullroarer.

The general interpretation of the myth rests on the symbolism of the monsoon season, regarded as a time of fructification. Julunggul is the male principle in nature, even though there is also a female manifestation; and the myth cycle concerns the increase of human and other creatures, including plants. The problem of dual sexuality is an interesting one, especially in regard to mythical Snakes such as the Rainbow (see Warner 1937/58: 383-4; R. Berndt 1951a: 24-5). It is one aspect of the male-female dialogue that permeates so much of myth and ritual in Aboriginal Australia.

The ritual counterpart of the Wawalag cycle is the *djunggawon*. Spencer (1914: 144-6) speaks of the Jungoan (i.e., *djunggawon*) for the Kakadu of western Arnhem Land: but the local people of that area do not perform it now, and, except for 'totemic' dancing, Spencer's description has little resemblance to the eastern Arnhem Land version. In the last, novices are taken from their mothers to a secluded place, or taken to visit other areas. On their return to the home camp, *wangidja* posts representing the Wawalag are erected in a clearing. Men cluster round these, singing parts of the Wawalag cycle; women dance round them too. Some distance away, on the secret-sacred ground, a triangular space is cleared, symbolizing the body of Julunggul, and at one end a hole represents Muruwul. Ritual dances are performed there, some of which are revealed to novices. The Julunggul drone-pipe (didjeri-du) is brought out from its shelter and blown over the heads of uninitiated boys and youths who have gone through only the preliminary stages of the *djunggawon*; they are covered with the sacred *ngainmara* conical mats (see hereunder). Blood, taken from the arm-veins of initiated men, is used as an adhesive for the feather-down decorating the dancers' bodies. The blood represents the blood of the Wawalag which attracted the attention of Julunggul—who (in the form of the drone-pipe) moves round the secret-sacred ground. Later, novices are painted with sacred patterns and, with the other men, return to the main camp for the actual circumcision rite. Surrounded by a tight ring of men hiding them from view, they are cut while women dance round them calling out ritually. Final rites concern the steaming of the novices, and the return of Julunggul to the sacred water-hole.

For girls, the procedure is much simpler. At puberty there is a brief seclusion period; the girl is red-ochred and decorated with a *maidga* breast harness. Interestingly, in this context, traditionally she was permitted to move about only with the help of two digging sticks, in the style of walking sticks; the mythical analogy here refers to the two Djangga-wul sisters, who used *rangga* pole emblems in that way.

In western Arnhem Land, among Gunwinggu and Maung, the major ritual sequences are the *ubar* and the *maraiin*: a third, the *kunapipi*, has been introduced within the last thirty years or so. The *ubar* is primarily initiatory, although it may also be performed without the presence of novices, or without novices participating in it for the first time. The *ubar* was first reported by Spencer (1914:133-44); but although the ritual he describes is very close to the Oenpelli and Goulburn Islands versions, the only references he provides to mythic associations concern an 'old man kangaroo' (*ibid.*: 138-40) and Ngabadaua (presumably Yirawadbad). The *ubar* is primarily a fertility ritual, mythically substantiated through a number of interconnected accounts. One primary figure here is Ngaljod the Rainbow Snake or, in her guise as Mother, Waramurunggundji. Initially she refused to circumcise youths, but instituted girls' puberty rites. (Circumcision and subincision are known to this area but are not traditional: see R. Berndt 1952*a*; 1952*b*.) The main origina-tor of the *ubar* ritual as such was Yirawadbad the Snake-man (see R. and C. Berndt 1970: 117-21, 128-32, 230-3), who showed this to Nadulmi (the large male kangaroo). The central ritual object is the hollow *ubar* log (or drum), a combined Mother symbol and Snake symbol which has its counterpart in the eastern Arnhem Land *uwar* (*ngurlmag* ritual: see Warner 1937/58: 311-29).

This ritual sequence commences at the beginning of the wet season, and emphasizes the female principle much more than does Julunggul in the *djunggawon*. However, Ngaljod and Julunggul can be either male or female, depending on context. A secret-sacred ground is prepared and symbolizes the Mother's body; the men who enter it are said to be going into the Mother's uterus; novices are 'swallowed' by her. The *ubar* log is also the Mother, and the sound it makes when hit is her voice. When they hear this, women in the main camp answer by calling out, *Gaidba, gaidba*! Novices are brought to the ground by their guardians, and a series of rites takes place. In one, a pair of novices sit one at each end of the *ubar*. As each side in turn is lifted up, an object within it (the beating-stump) rolls down and touches the hands of the novice. This re-enacts the mythic scene when Yirawadbad, in his poisonous snake manifestation, bit his wife and her mother, killing them both. Novices are then shown various dramatic acts. Finally, all leave the ground and return to the main camp, where two women climb up a forked post and swing *lida* shell rattles, while other women dance around it, and men, in their turn, climb the forked post and call sacred invocations,

Gunwinggu ritual in general is graded in a series of stages. Novices begin at the first and move through fairly uniformly. Each subsequent ritual is regarded as a reinforcement of the previous one, and each is designed to extend the knowledge and experience of those participating (R. and C. Berndt 1970: 234). Over and above ritual as a learning process, enhancing both religious and social status, is its purpose in more general terms. In western Arnhem Land, no physical operation is performed on either boys or girls: puberty rites for girls are straightforward and, as for boys, food tabus are significant (and can be said to take the place of physical operations). The Rainbow Snake is relevant in this context too, and a menstruating girl must not attract his (her) attention. She is red-ochred at the completion of her seclusion period, a crescent moon is painted in white below her breasts to regulate her menses, and sometimes the Rainbow itself is painted between her breasts (R. and C. Berndt 1964/68: 153-4).

Spencer (1914: 88-176) has provided descriptive accounts of initiation patterns over a fairly wide area. For variations in circumcision rites, see also Elkin (1938/64: 66:7) and R. and C. Berndt (*ibid.*: fig. 10, 139).

On Groote Eylandt (Turner 1970), the main focus of initiation is (was until recently) circumcision, along with admission into the Babara ritual when a youth begins to grow a beard. The Babara is a specialized mortuary or remembrance ritual associated with a 'culture hero' named Blaur (see under iii. *Death*). Further instructional rituals were held (that is, teaching a circumcised youth his local group song cycle), as well as cicatrization. Additionally, the circumcisional *mandiwala* (equivalent to the *djunggawon*) has been introduced to Groote from the mainland. As far as is known, there were no puberty rites for females.

The Tiwi are an example of a group which, like the Gunwinggu and Maung, has no physical operation associated with initiation (except depilation): but unlike them, the Tiwi make no sexual distinctions on the sacred ground. Spencer (1914: 91-115) describes the *kulama*, as have other writers (for example, Hart and Pilling 1960: 93-5, and C. P. Mountford 1958: 122-30). Comments here are taken mainly from M. Brandl (1971). The *kulama* is substantiated by mythology involving several spirit beings, the 'first' initiates being Jirakati (whiteheaded sea-eagle) and Tupatupini (a small owl). The Ningaui spirit people are said to have performed the second *kulama*, which focuses on the *kulama* yams and their preparation as food.

In the past, such initiation was relevant to both men and women, but in recent years it has shifted to involve mainly men, although women do take part. The rites themselves are conducted by fully initiated men who enter a state of *pukumani*. This word can best be described as meaning 'sacred' or 'forbidden', and will be referred to again later. Here it means that the main participants have to observe various tabus before and during the *kulama*. In the past, initiates were *pukumani* for up to seven years. The *kulama* is regarded as a dangerous-sacred plant. The rituals are commenced toward the end of the wet season. The yams are gathered and kept in a special shelter. Later they are prepared, cooked, rubbed on the bodies of male and female participants, and finally eaten. The ritual sequences include much singing and dancing, body decoration, and a number of subsidiary actions. Mountford (1958: 131) notes how small portions of the *juruguni* and *karawani* (long and short yams) are chewed and spat out to make the *mopadili* (spirits of the dead) sick so that they will leave the *kulama*. In another rite, water from a bark container is squirted into the air to imitate rain, along with the sound of thunder: or a bark basket is hit to make the same sound (*ibid.*: 133). Once the *kulama* are removed from ovens and cut up, they are rubbed on the bodies of men, women and children. Men slice some of them and mash them with red-ochre, rubbing this substance into their hair and over their bodies. Tiwi believe that this prevents sickness, and that the rubbing in general is physically strengthening (*ibid.*: 138). Initiands are decorated with cane rings, hair-string belts and goose-feather balls. Although the tangible, visible focus is on yams, it is obvious that these stand for or symbolize a range of natural phenomena, some of which are expressly stated, others merely implied. It is as if the dangerous-sacred yam has the power which triggers off the monsoonal period and stimulates all growth. However, M. Brandl (1971) notes that the *kulama* is performed toward the *end* of the wet season and that one interpretation could be the control of the rains, preventing their extension over a long period, and so avoiding floods. (See M. Brandl 1970, for a discussion of the *kulama* in the past and in the present.)

Whichever way we look at the *kulama*, the welfare of the group is seen to be inherent in, symbolized by, the yam itself, and it stands in relation to all Tiwi in those terms: through the ritual focusing on it, the normal sequence of events, natural and social, can be maintained. This view is crystallized in the belief that if the *kulama* is broken it can harm individual persons and also the group as a whole. The yam is dangerous, and is treated with great care. It is regarded, in effect, as a sacred object: if it is broken in digging, or in other circumstances, 'the spirit of sickness [may be] released by the angry yam' (Mountford 1958: 134); uncooked yams are placed in water to make them 'quiet' (to counteract their dangerous qualities); the yams are carefully placed in the oven and covered while cooking, otherwise their power could escape and cause blindness.

On the mainland in western Arnhem Land, the ritual centring on the *mangindjeg* root (Gundjeibmi, R. and C. Berndt 1970: 132-3) is roughly comparable but was never, as far as we know, elaborated to such an extent as among the Tiwi. Spencer (1914: 146-9) provides a Kakadu example which he called the *kulori* ceremony. On the Daly River, the Ngulugwongga focused on a goose-egg rite which was diffused symbolically to include general fertility and seasonal increase: it preceded circumcision (see R. and C. Berndt 1964/68: 146-7). Stanner (1933: 10-4; 1959-61: 80-9) has referred to initiation rites in the Daly River-Port Keats areas. Novices were taken on a journey to other territories, and during that period had to observe various tabus, Finally they were returned to their own country and circumcised. Ritual washing took place, with the enforcement of a period of silence, and dramatized rites were carried out at regular intervals during this whole time. Puberty rites for girls (as among the Ngulugwongga, Madngala, Wogiman and Nangiomeri: see R. and C. Berndt 1964/68: 154) were associated with the Rainbow. A girl was ritually bathed, and food was collected and placed in a mound, over which she stepped; when she sat down it was piled around her; later, it was distributed. On the whole, the process was less elaborate for girls; but there was seclusion, with ritual washing concluding the period: also, food and gift exchanges took place at the breaking of silence for male and for female novices.

Basedow (1907: 10-6) provides information on Laragia (Larakia) and Wogaidj initiation. The Laragia did not circumcise, although the Wogaidj did; and the Laragia had a relatively elaborate ritual for girls at puberty, involving ritual washing and 'smoking'.

Stanner (1959-61: 109-27), however, emphasizes as well the post-circumcisional rites relevant to the *karwadi* (*kalwadi*), which include the bullroarer: this is the ritual which the Murinbata call *punj*. Certainly such rites are initiatory, but they are also other things. For instance, all religious rituals involve the acceptance, or potential acceptance, of certain persons who have not yet seen them, and one intention is to teach and/or incorporate such persons in a sense of commitment. However, in this context, it is preferable to think of initiation as representing the first exposure to the formal world of religion. Stanner reports the intent of the *karwadi* as 'making the young men understand', and if that is so it can perhaps be accepted as being initiatory. At the same time, he does say that it 'is not *only* an initiation'. (Stanner provides a descriptive and interpretative analysis which we will not go into here.) The rituals take place on a secret-sacred ground, where the youths are gathered together with the men: they sing, and the songs focus on *karwadi*, symbolizing the Mother.

Briefly, the sequence includes conventionalized jesting between particular relatives (the *tjirmumuk*); the removal of the youths' social and, indeed, human identity; they are told they will be swallowed by Karwadi (as Mother) and regurgitated; they are smeared with blood (from the Mother); and dramatic performances are held. On the third day, the *karwadi* bullroarers are heard and seen, and initiates learn where the blood comes from. Potential wives' brothers of the initiates bring forward the bullroarers and rub them on the youths' bodies, and thrust them between their thighs so that they stand erect like a penis. Finally, the youths are re-anointed with blood and provided with a headband and hairbelt, among other things. All return to the main camp, where the youths crawl between the legs of initiated men toward their mothers, while all the women wail as in mourning: the youths return, between the legs of the men, in the same way. There are also various prohibitions. After a week, the youths are again decorated with a bullroarer design said not to be identified by women. This signals their new status, and after a lapse of two years they are permitted to marry.

As noted, the interpretation of these rites is the subject of Stanner's papers (*ibid.*), and in these he sets out the supporting mythology. Circumcision, he says (*ibid.*: 250), 'is not a secret, obscure and dangerous thing. Its purpose is to make a youth into a man, whereas the purpose of the rite of the bullroarer is to make a man into a man of mystical understanding'. He draws a distinction between circumcision rites, concerned with 'the highest secular values' and the bullroarer rite, concerned with 'highest religious values' (*ibid.*: 81). Obviously, there is a difference here between induction and indoctrination. Or, to put it another way, between the acceptance of a candidate for 'higher' studies and that candidate's actual involvement in ritual affairs. Or, again, the contrast between receptivity and actual acceptance. However, the contrast between secular and religious values is less real since both rest on a similar structure of symbolic statement: in both, in the rites of circumcision and in the manipulation of bullroarers, men re-enact what are considered to be basic truths; both are religious, and both lead toward 'understanding' and do not confer under-standing *per se*. There are some interesting problems here: for example, the real penis in one (that is, it is circumcised) and the symbolic penis (that is, the bullroarer) in the other. Additionally, the complementary interplay of male (bullroarer) and female (Mother) elements suggest that other things are being done besides the 'routine' of circumcision and besides the conferring of sacred status on the bullroarer novices.

In the central west of the Northern Territory, among the Walbiri (Meggitt 1962: 281-316), initiation rites consist of circumcision (at about 12 years of age) and subincision (at 16 or 17 years of age). A seclusion camp for novices is established, where they are placed in the charge of a guardian, and it is here that many of the dramatic performances (as revelatory rituals) are held. These include the painting of designs on shields by the 'workers' (men of the patrimoiety opposite the one to which a particular novice belongs); the patterns are relevant to the novices' patrimoieties. The 'masters' (that is, men of a novice's patri-moiety) choose several Dreamings that are important to a novice's country—but not the Dreaming of his own 'lodge' or local group, into which he is being initiated. The painted shields are displayed and relevant Dreaming rites follow, which uncircumcised novices do not see. They do, however, listen to mythological song sequences in the main camp, while men sing and women dance. At this time, the close 'mothers' (actual and classificatory) of the novices surround them and their guardian, brandishing firesticks.

(Traditionally, novices would then go on a tour of the country, visiting many different Walbiri areas and issuing invitations to attend the circumcision; in turn, they were given hairstring. After that, they would return to the seclusion camp.)

A ritual ground is prepared, and the novices are told the mythological meaning of the rites they witness there; in this context, these are predominantly of the Kangaroo Dream-ing. Older men prepare the long incised *jarandalba* boards, rubbing them with red-ochre and singing over them. A novice's mother's brother makes a small *windilburu* bullroarer and incises on it the boy's conception Dreaming design, to be given to him after circumcision. Each evening there are ritual gatherings near the main camp, where sacred songs are sung and women dance: and there too a novice's mother dances, holding a firebrand. Also, he is taken by the women to another clearing where his face and neck are rubbed with a kangaroo leg bone to make him strong and tall, and they wail over him. Eventually he is returned to the men. The women run in single file along the main clearing: male Kangaroo singers rush at them, and they run screaming to the camp. Every evening the women dance a little farther down the clearing, the far end of which is to be used for the actual rite. After a final Kangaroo rite, songs of the Emu Dreaming are sung; women sit behind the men, and the *windilburu* is swung; everyone, including the novices, sees this. Subsidiary rites at this stage include novices jumping over a fire, to induce growth; the *jagingiri* fire chanting, with the chasing of the women from the ground to the accompaniment of hurling coals and burning brands; and the removal of the novices by the women. Men swing a bullroarer, sing the special *widi* songs (referring to poles carried by Dreaming initiated men), and select ritual dancers. The *jarandalba* boards are inspected and taken to a bough-shelter. During the night, while most of the camp sleeps, the novices are shown the *jarandalba* of their fathers' 'lodges' by their brothers, and the significance of the markings is explained to them. Men patrol the area, swinging bullroarers to warn others to keep away. Spears (representing their penes) are made for the novices, and hanks of hairstring (representing pubic hair) are prepared for them. About this time, too, a novice's mother again dances with a firebrand which represents her son's old life: it is extinguished when he is circumcised. Meggitt (*ibid.*: 294) emphasizes that 'he dies only to be reborn', and that the Walbiri 'explicitly equate circumcision with ritual killing'.

Later, blood is removed from penis-incisures for use as an adhesive to decorate the bodies of novices with feather-down. Then *jarandalba* boards are displayed, while women sit with covered heads: the boards, held upright, are said to represent erect penes. The *windilburu* bullroarer is swung and then put in the sand near the novice's head and, since it bears his conception totem design, its virtue enters him. Large *wanigi* (string or thread crosses) are made, on a basis of specially selected *jarandalba* boards, and arm blood is spurted on them and over the *windilburu* bullroarers. There is also a penis-holding rite (see R. Berndt 1965: 187-90). Finally, the circumcisional rites are held in the main clearing. Novices perform a hopping Kangaroo dance to demonstrate their acquisition of ritual knowledge. Then fires are lit and the *widi* dancing commences. During this, the novices' eyes are shielded and women bow their heads while a large *wanigi* is displayed. The novices are told to look up, and each of them is lifted by two of his brothers toward this emblem, which is pressed against him. Women are then driven from the ground, and the circumcisers dance up to the novices and strike them with the poles. The *wanigi* is placed toward the opposite end of the clearing; there is further dancing; the *widi* poles are set aflame; and several men form a table on which each novice lies while his foreskin is removed and thrown into a fire. At the same time, the novices' mothers extinguish their torches (*ibid.*: 304). The novices are carried back to the other men and further dancing follows. They are shown the *wanigi*. Bullroarers are swung, and given to them. They are also given the *wanigi* to handle, and again it is pressed to their chests: in this way, a novice is told, the 'lodge' patri-spirit enters him.

These rites do not lend themselves to the kind of distinction Stanner drew for Port Keats. The circumcisional sequences described by Meggitt have close parallels at Wave Hill and Birrundudu, except that ritual death is not so strongly emphasized there. Meggitt notes several times that the boy is said to be 'killed': for example, a novice's father embraces the circumcisers 'to show that he bears no animosity towards the killer of his son'; a novice's mother extinguishes her torch—'her son is dead'; the *widi* poles strike a novice 'to single him out as the intended victim of the killing' (*ibid.*: 303-4), and so on. Notwithstanding such comments, the focus is on life, on acquiring knowledge, and on demonstrating this (when the novice 'hops' like a kangaroo). In all cases, it is the power of ritual dancing and the emblems that are used which express this. Moreover, a novice's own conception Dreaming (as spirit) is there and is 'given to' him to a signify once more a re-union or re-affirmation of his pre-natal sacredness. With this, the spirit of his father's local group ('lodge'), associated with a segment of a major myth-ritual sequence, enters and becomes part of him. Throughout the whole initiation process, myth and the Dreamings are ever-present; and the role of women is a significant one, even though it is not at the executive level.

Subincision is a further stage of initiation in this area (*ibid.*: 310-16). But prior to this, and after his circumcision, a youth is admitted to his first *gadjari* (see hereunder). At that time, he is permitted to witness further rituals of his local group, some of them of an increase nature. A subincision initiand is rubbed all over with red-ochre, and taken to the secret-sacred ground. There the relevant songs are sung and dramatic acts performed. As the sun rises, the initiand is placed on his back and incised. In sympathy for him, certain female relatives in the main camp may cicatrize themselves. The subincised youth remains secluded until his penis is healed. Usually, in the adjacent Wave Hill area, older men open their incisures at the same time as the initiand is cut and perform special dancing: the movement causes their loins and legs to be sprinkled with blood from the wound. Symbolically, this is menstrual blood.

The central west of the Northern Territory is a general label for a wide area covering many pastoral stations and the Hooker's Creek region considered by Meggitt, and abutting on this is the Desert immediately to the south, stretching west and south-west into Western Australia. In this region, Aboriginal women have their own secret-sacred rites, as well as those (such as circumcision) in which they participate with men. Two primary cycles are involved: the *djarada* and the *jawalju* (yawalyu). The first, the more northern variety, extends east and northeast to the Roper River and Arnhem Land; the second is the Desert form (see C. Berndt 1950a: 11-85; also 1965: 238-82). The rules governing inclusion and exclusion (who is admitted, or not admitted, and to what) are not identical over the entire region, as regards either their content or their flexibility in practice. They are fairly consistent in excluding men of all ages, except in special circumstances (e.g., as a patient in a healing rite), but differ in regard to children, and even in regard to younger women. They differ also in their range of paraphernalia as well as body designs. Sanctions for breaches of the rules do not rest on human agents. Punishment is believed to follow almost automatically: because of their associations with the supernatural, with the realm of the sacred, the rites and songs and their visible representations are dangerous to unauthorized persons. For this reason, they complement the great fertility cults and/or the rituals performed by specific local groups.

Kaberry (1939: 78-83) has discussed both male initiation and women's secret-sacred 'ceremonies'. She emphasizes the part played by women. One point, which underlines complementarity in this context, is what she calls the *yoelyu* 'corroboree' (referred to by C. Berndt 1950a; 27, note 19, as being probably the *jaludju* [yaludju], which is a normal part of the circumcision ritual), in which a novice's mother-in-law carries a firestick 'to make him grow up, to make him into a man so that he can marry' (*ibid.*: 82). Her explanation here differs from Meggitt's (see above). Kaberry (*ibid.*: 97-100) also mentions, as C. Berndt did, a potential husband taking a certain type of sacred board (*munguana*) and singing songs to make his betrothed's breasts develop and her pubic hair grow (Djaru, east Kimberley). Wolmeri women's secret ritual did focus on female puberty, and at one time introcision was practised—as a counterpart to male subincision. In one sense, the aim of both male and female puberty ritual is the same—to hasten on social adulthood enabling both to play a more active part in social affairs, including religious matters.

In the Balgo area of the southern Kimberleys, there is no formal instruction for girls at puberty. But for boys the situation of freedom from responsibilities changes rapidly at initiation. A boy is seized and taken to a seclusion camp, as a *malulu*, a novice. As in the Walbiri case, a novice was initially taken by his prospective circumcisers on a pilgrimage to various sacred sites. At such a time, he was shown the visible and tangible evidence of mythic activity and expected to learn the relevant mythology. It is important to emphasize that all initiation ritual, including the novice's journey, is said to replicate similar events associated with mythic beings in the Dreaming era. This is the past as a model for the present, a theme significant to virtually all ritual. In terms of management, two groups of people are concerned in an initiation sequence. One comprises the 'active' and executive members (for example, a novice's prospective parents-in-law and brothers-in-law and his grandparents). The others (mainly the novice's own parents, brothers and actual cross-cousins) have the more passive role of wailing for the novice and preparing gifts for initiators. During the circumcisional proceedings, women and children come on to the sacred ground and dance: the novice is regarded as being ritually dead, or suspended, awaiting emergence into adult life. Finally, women and children return to the main camp, and circumcision follows. Immediately afterward, as among the Walbiri, the boy is given his first bullroarer (*darugu*, a general word meaning sacred or 'set apart' but also used for such objects), its designs representing the country associated with his 'conception' and local group Dreaming (*djarin-djugur*: see above). From this juncture, until his subincision, a youth is known as *bugudi*. Shortly after his circumcision, he participates in a blood rite: he is given arm blood to drink—which links his life with that of the sacred beings as well as with initiated men: blood equals life, and mythic power is contained in it. Some blood is spurted over him. Various rites are performed, during which sacred boards and other objects are displayed—but at this early stage he is not permitted to look at them, and must remain covered. It is only after subincision that he is shown the 'higher' revelatory rites, along with the sacred boards and, especially, the 'thread cross' hair-string object (*wanigi*). Like the Walbiri, the people now centred on Balgo (Gugadja-Walmadjeri) do not permit a youth to marry until he is subincised.

Initiation rites vary (see Elkin 1938/64: 202-13 and R. and C. Berndt 1964/68: 136-57).

To look at another example, initiation sequences in the Broome-Sunday Island area included tooth-evulsion and circumcision, among other rites, and seven basic stages were delineated before a novice was classified as a man. Piddington (1932: 46-87) writes of Kara-djeri initiation as comprising two traditions, the 'southern' and the 'northern'. The first is substantiated by the Bagadjimbiri mythology associated with the travels of two brothers, typical of a great deal of the mythology of this area. At the sites they visited, the brothers witnessed or carried out certain actions which gave those places their particular sacredness. At Injidan Pool, for example, they saw a number of women digging for locusts: this therefore became an increase centre for locusts. They also shaped male and female genitals, and instituted the first circumcisional rituals, making the *galiguru* bullroarer and the large *birmal* boards, and on these they incised intricate patterning which depicted their own travels. The actual circumcisional rituals of this tradition resemble those noted briefly for Balgo. A *malulu* novice is wailed over by his relatives and attends a number of preliminary rites, including an exchange of vegetable food between the novice's local group and visitors. Novices witness a number of dramatic performances, and during the singing of songs referring to the *midedi* (or *mididi*) feast (see later) they are covered with bushes. Blood is later removed from arm veins on the secret-sacred ground and they drink this from a bark dish. Blood is also smeared over their bodies, and they are sprinkled with powdered charcoal. A ritual meal takes place in the main camp, and the novice is given a lighted firestick by (usually) his father's mother. This firestick is to light the fire in which his circumcised penis is to be warmed for healing. The novice then sets out on a journey, accompanied by a party of men: he carries his firestick, which is replaced from time to time. On his return to the home group he enters in single file with a long line of visitors. Again he is decorated with blood: there is a gift of boomerangs from the visitors, and food is provided by the hosts. The novices are then removed to the *yuna* ground, where they are circumcised, and during this time various mythic dances are performed. Afterward they are given presents, and bullroarers are swung.

The mythology of 'the northern tradition', to use Piddington's label, is much more extensive and, as he observes, includes a number of mythic beings responsible for instituting sections of the total initiation complex. Some of these are known in the Balgo area. One of those specifically concerning initiation is Milyanganabunggan, an old man who killed and ate boys; he was tracked down by their mothers who, with the boys' help, killed him. 'Thus arose the tradition that at initiation boys are not killed but merely circumcised' (*ibid.*: 59). In another, *Kamida* (Goanna) had two sons who were eventually circumcised by others in his absence. As a result he became angry and made a fire in which everyone perished except himself and his sons; but the fire was so hot that they had to seek refuge in a pool south-east of La Grange, where they were metamorphosed as stones. A variation of this fire theme is noted in R. Berndt (1971) for the Walmadjeri-Gugadja: in that case, it took place at Lake White and relates to the Ganabuḍa in the *dingari* cycle (see below). In the northern circumcisional ritual (*wolawola*), a major feature is dancing by women who call out their 'totem' (Dreaming) names as they move across the ground, and as the men call theirs. Later the boy is circumcised, arm blood is drunk, and dancing of the *miruru* spirits is shown to him, in the course of which the actors spurt blood over him. A bullroarer is swung, and is then given to him. Finally, the intitate is returned to the main camp, to the sound of swinging bullroarers.

Petri and Petri-Odermann (1970: 252, 261-2) provide additional material on initiation and the *worgaia* tradition at La Grange. Petri (1968: 270-1) discusses the various initiation grades among the Njulnjul (Nyulnyul) and the western Kimberleys generally (*ibid.*: Chapter III, 265-74), including the Ungarinyin, Worora and Unambal (Petri 1954: 217-29). See also Petri (1960a: 133-45), Worms (1938), Elkin (1936) and Lommel (1949; 1952), as well as Craig (1968) for bibliographical references for the Kimberleys.

In this summarized outline, initiation is treated at two levels. Over and above increased status for the novices concerned (both male and female), including a period of disciplining and learning which is viewed as an introduction to what will become a new and exciting adult life, there is the separation from women and children, as a convention which explicitly spells out changes in responsibility. This does not represent a breaking away from what might be interpreted as a mundane area of social life. At the first level, then, is the ritual treatment of a novice who is removed temporarily from the mainstream of social activity while at the same time becoming the central focus of that actitivy. Ritual 'death' is a common thread throughout, and this is expressed through a novice's removal from the main camp: even though he occasionally returns to it at different initiatory junctures, he is not separated from his guardians—or if he is, the separation is of a ritual nature. In nearly all areas considered here, the novice, after being taken from the main camp and introduced to the secret-sacred ground, is said to be swallowed—by Julunggul, Ngaljod, the Mother, the Rainbow Snake (see Radcliffe-Brown *et al.* 1931: 3-16), or Ungud (Petri 1968 and Worms 1938), or by some other mythic being. The sound of the twirling bullroarer is the voice of the mythic being who calls the men to the secret-sacred ground *and* swallows the novice. Meanings vary. In some cases, the mythic presence at such a ritual is female or male (or both). In north-eastern Arnhem Land, the novices represent the Wawalag sisters who are swallowed by Julunggul: the blood on their bodies is symbolically menstrual and/or afterbirth blood. Blood, in virtually all instances, signifies 'life'. Stanner makes the point that the blood smeared over the novice is that of the Mother—it is life-sustaining: and in some cases, blood is drunk (or sipped) to co-join the novice's life with that of the mythic beings and participants. The ritual death of the novice and his 'killing' receives emphasis in the initiation rituals reported (for example) by Meggitt, but it is counterbalanced by life-giving ritual.

At the second level of interpretation, ritual 'death' can be seen not simply as death but as a *transformation*. (I am using 'transformation' in a way different from Munn 1970: 153-4; but see her discussion of this in relation to Walbiri initiation. What is significant in this context is her statement that '... ancestral transformation has associations with notions of death and birth ...') This analogy is reinforced through the symbolism of the swallowing by mythic beings. In virtually all cases, the novice is said to remain 'alive' within that being: he is not 'killed' by it, but is transformed both physically and spiritually. This is explicitly stated in the symbolism of the fertility cults in which postulants (and novices) enter the secret-sacred ground. At such a time, it is said, they are entering the Mother's uterus. However, where transformation is concerned, the Dreaming must be kept in mind. Many mythic beings were shape-changing in the course of their bodily existence in the creative era. When, later, they were killed or met their death in some way, or simply disappeared into the ground, into a site or waterhole, and so on, they were transformed without detracting in any way from their essential character. Aboriginal man is believed to possess this same quality—except that in his case these are ritual transformations, not spontaneous 'natural' Dreaming changes as was the case with the mythic beings.

In these forms of initiation, male-female collaboration is an essential ingredient. Certainly, 'secular' values are being reinforced and ratified, but so are those which in a different form are expressed in so-called 'higher' varieties of religious ritual. What should be made clear, though, is that the distinction between secular and other values is mostly in terms of symbolic layers—the wrapping up of basic social and natural facts in a series of symbolic statements.

Over and above the mechanics of initiation, there is recognition that human beings are manipulating powers which transcend those available in everyday life; that these powers, or forces, can be dangerous to certain categories of persons; and that they can be handled only on a ritual basis, by fully initiated persons who have placed themselves firmly within and identified themselves with the Dreaming. It is in the way these powers are dealt with, that male-female participation can be defined. They are mainly handled by men because, the Aborigines generally contend, men are better able to cope with such dangerous things. In the Tiwi *kulama* example, however, *both* sexes are involved in this, in controlling and channelizing forces which can bring harmful as well as beneficent results.

Essentially, however, in ritual action as in mythic belief, the interplay between male and female attributes is seen as being complementary, and not necessarily as being antagonistic. It is true that certain myths suggest antipathy between the sexes. But where this is expressed, it is seen mainly as a natural condition within a broader frame where the emphasis is on harmony. It is often a matter of varying sex roles, and their corresponding expectations. The bullroarer is a case in point; so are the *jarandalba* boards, displayed by men as erect penes. These portray a male attribute which is seen as symbolizing the relations between the sexes. At the same time, its connotations are much wider than this.

Further, the bullroarer is an outward expression of a man's own local group Dreaming. The incisings on it do not in all areas depict a person's conception Dreaming. Nevertheless, in most it symbolizes a mythic linkage between that person and his Dreaming, specifically noted or diffused, as referring to a mythic sponsor of an initiation ritual. A point to remember here is that not all bullroarers are male symbols: some are female.

iii. *Death*

Death is treated as merely a further transformation, although the matter is not always put so simply. The finality of physical death is rationalized through an acceptance of this as a natural and inevitable state of affairs. At the same time, there is a firm belief that the spirit of man is released from its mundane trappings to enable it to take another shape. Accepting the belief that a human body must be spiritually animated at birth, and that the 'force' which does this comes from the Dreaming, it is reasonable to accept that, on death, this same 'force' returns to the Dreaming. In R. and C. Berndt (1964/68: 183) two diagrams summarize the main features in the life cycle of men and women, one for north-eastern Arnhem Land, the other for the Western Desert. Although these vary from one area to another, the 'beginning' and the 'end' of life are, essentially, not so different. In both cases, ritual actions are necessary to ensure that the spirit enters or is removed from ordinary life—bringing it out of the Dreaming, and setting it on its way back to the Dreaming. The procedures used to achieve this and the beliefs that underlie them are by no means uniform, any more than are those concerned with the spiritual animation of the foetus, or with initiation into social adulthood.

In one sense, mortuary ritual constitutes a person's last involvement in the human physical aspect of living. All sacred ritual activity can be seen as leading to death, and mortuary ritual as a person's last sacred ritual. Further, the nearer he (or she) is to death, the more sacred (again, in one sense) a person becomes—and this is not solely because of his (or her) increased involvement in sacred matters. It is also because at or near death one is, again, being drawn inevitably into the realm of the sacred or the Dreaming.

The most complex mortuary rituals are those of north-eastern Arnhem Land and Bathurst and Melville Islands. Warner (1937/58: 412-50) has a detailed description of these among the 'Murngin'. The first ritual, he says, demonstrates the intent of the whole. A large sand or ground pattern of the deceased's country, including his 'conception well', is constructed to one side of the main camp. (See plate facing p. 175 in R. and C. Berndt 1965.) Songs are sung around this, specifically those centring on the deceased's own mythic associations, and the sacred names of his waterhole and country are invoked. In Warner's words, 'the names of the totems are sung to enable the dying [or dead] man to act like his totem and become like it, that is, to be completely spiritualized . . .' (*ibid.*: 443). The songs, moreover, direct his spirit. Two concepts are involved. One, through properly handled ritual, the spirit is 'translated back to the world of the dead'; but since the deceased has been 'magically' killed (as Warner notes, many deaths in this region are attributed to sorcery—not all, but an appreciable number), he is dangerous: and a series of purificatory rites is necessary to sever the dead from the living. Be this as it may, a further interpretation rests on the deceased's spirit and all associated with it as being sacred—both dangerous and neutral, in the same way that, for example, initiation ritual can be 'dangerous' to specific categories of person and must consequently be handled with ritual care. The rites surrounding the disposal of the corpse (which is really incidental, since it is the 'disposal' or removal of the deceased's spirit which is of crucial concern) are designed 'to combat the disturbing effects of the death and, particularly, to bring pressure to bear on that aspect of the dead man's spirit which was believed to cling to its earthly home' (see R. Berndt 1965: 200). And the ritual songs 'help the spirit to merge with the eternal Dreaming (*wongar*) stream and to enter the Land of the Dead'.

Over and above the arranging of a corpse on a platform for decomposition and eventual bone collection (the traditional practice in north-eastern Arnhem Land), mortuary rituals are held spasmodically over a period of years, and not only in the locality where the death occurred. When the bones are collected, they are red-ochred and placed in a bark coffin. Later, in a ritual context, some are broken up and hidden in a long hollow log, which has been shaped as a mythic creature in 'totemic' form and painted in emblemic designs signifying the deceased's country and his mythic associations. Some of the bones, with the skull (in one part of this area, also traditionally painted in sacred clan patterns), are placed in the deceased's waterhole and/or carried about by a widow or widower for some time. There are variations on this theme, and much depends on the deceased's clan and moiety. In the *jiridja* moiety, masts and flags are used to farewell the spirit; and a *wuramu*, a wooden post-figure representing the deceased's earthly image or a mythic or pseudo-historical character, is made and set up in the camp.

Each moiety has its own Land of the Dead, with related mythology, and that Land is a central focus in the songs and rites surrounding and following a death. For the *dua* moiety it is the mythical island of Bralgu, somewhere in the Gulf of Carpentaria; it was from here that the Djanggawul set off on their journey to the Australian mainland, although in one version this was not their original home but merely a halting place on their way. For the *jiridja* it is Mudilnga, an unidentified island north-east of the Wessel Islands, sometimes identified with the Torres Strait Islands or the southern New Guinea coast under the collective name of 'Badu' (R. Berndt 1948a: 93-103; R. and C. Berndt 1964/68: 415-18).

One problem here is the divisibility of the deceased's soul or spirit. Warner speaks of two souls: one, the *birimbir* and the other the *mogwoi* (Warner 1937/58: 445-50), although the former may also divide. The *mogwoi* is locally and territorially bound and remains outside the main Dreaming stream, but is eventually submerged within a general category of malignant spirits—which do, in fact, have their origin in the Dreaming. The *birimbir* is the 'true' eternal spirit of man: one aspect of it returns to the deceased's well or waterhole to await rebirth, while its other aspect travels to the appropriate Land of the Dead where it will eventually be united with the *wongar* beings and merged within the Dreaming. The significant fact here is the sacred quality of the *birimbir* of both men and women. As Warner notes (*ibid.*: 280-1), the spirits of the dead are believed to be *in* the sacred *rangga* emblems used in secret-sacred ritual: 'If my older brother should die, next Narra [*nara*] or Djungguan [*djunggawon*] we have, he would come back and go in that ranga [*rangga*] ...' 'The little babies when they are fish [unborn] live in the same place with marikmo [*marimo*, father's father] and mari [mother's mother's brother] souls'. Or, again, 'Even though "spirits go to the islands of the dead, or the whale takes them to the Warumeri well [Waramiri *mada*, dialect unit], they come back to the ranga and go inside it and into the well".' And ' "When a woman dies she becomes Bir-im-bir [*birimbir*, spirit] Wongar [Dreaming] and goes to the same well as a man. She can come back to her ranga and is like those two old Wawilak sisters" [that is, the mythical Wawalag sisters, relevant to the *dua* moiety]'.

In the ideology of north-eastern Arnhem Land, the essential sacred quality of man and woman is unquestioned, as is the theme of cyclical transformation.

As far as western Arnhem Land is concerned, among Gunwinggu as among Maung, the ritual surrounding death parallels ritual for initiation. This ritual is called *lorgun*, of the delayed mortuary variety: but it may also be called *djunggawon* (see above, under ii. *Initiation*). It is substantiated by the Nagugur mythology; this father-son pair, responsible for instituting the *kunapipi* (see below), also sponsor the *lorgun*. It is further oriented round a version of a very widespread mythical theme. Djabo, a spotted cat, refused to drink Moon's urine, and thus deprived man of earthly immortality. (See R. and C. Berndt 1970: 133; another version appears in R. Berndt 1948*b* and R. and C. Berndt 1964/68: 336.)

Some sections of the *lorgun* are secret-sacred. With the waning moon, a close relative (father, brother or son) of the deceased constructs a sacred shelter within or just outside the main camp, and a long hollow log (the *lorgun*) is cut and decorated. When the proceedings begin, men dance decorated as for the secret-sacred *maraiin* rituals (see below), and novices who are present must observe food prohibitions. Then the log is brought out in the light of paperbark flares and the deceased's bones are unwrapped (after having been collected from the disposal platform), red-ochred and put into it. Later, the *lorgun* is erected in the main camp to the accompaniment of dancing: food is given to participants and there is an exchange of goods. One of the last songs sung tells of the deceased's spirit diving into the water, and invocations associated with his local group are called. Also, the deceased's clothing and possessions are burnt, and in the mound of ashes a post is placed. This is the *wawal*, which indicates that one aspect of the deceased's spirit can go to its own waterhole or country. Spencer (1914: 239-56) gives examples of Kakadu death rituals, and an outline of the Mangarei and Mara *lorgun*. Here too the secret-sacred aspect is stressed, the *lorgun* itself being decorated with the deceased's *maraiin* 'totemic' emblem. (Spencer [*ibid.*: 253-4] refers to the Mara eating a corpse: mortuary cannibalism was also carried out by the Maung [see R. and C. Berndt 1964/68: 400-3], but it was by no means general and will not be discussed here.) And Spencer notes (*ibid.*: 254-5) that a dead Mara man's spirit watches to see if his mourning ceremonies are carried out properly: when these are completed, his spirit goes to 'its original home in the far past times' (presumably, the Dreaming).

The evidence here supports the contention that the western Arnhem Landers (for example) consider death itself to be intimately connected with the sacred. One indication is its relevance as a secret-sacred ritual, and as a form of initiation with the acceptance of novices. At death, in this region too, the spirit of man is divisible: one part of it (the *maam* or *namandi*) remains near its earthly form, and is regarded as dangerous, almost anti-thetical to the persons and the life it has left, resenting its changed state. Another part, however, returns to its own country. In the *lorgun* the last song, as we have said, tells of the spirit diving into the water. This refers to the spirit entering a waterhole within its own country—which in turn is the place of its 'conception' or birth, linked to its paternal country: the invocations which follow the song emphasize this. However, the Gunwinggu and Maung each recognize a particular Land of the Dead, and the deceased's spirit, or part of it, is said to go there. (See R. and C. Berndt 1951: 107-8; 1964/68: 414-15.) For the Gunwinggu it is Manidjirangmad, a sky world; for the Maung, Wulurunbu Island, far out to sea and north-east of the Goulburn Islands. In both cases, the spirit or ghost meets various guardian beings who subject it to certain tests. After passing these, it is paddled by canoe across the water to the land of the ancestors, which includes the Dreaming beings.

On Groote Eylandt (Turner 1970), the same applies to spirits of the dead (called *wuramugwa*) as to the pre-natal spirit child. Turner remarks that, in a sense, these two opposite ends of the spirit continuum could be regarded as being more sacred than during the interim in between, when the spirit resides in the human body. When it is 'in residence', so to speak, it is called *awarawalja*, a word which means 'shade' or shadow. In this context, it is reasonable to suggest an emphasis on transition, on its changed status at birth, and its close identification with its pre-natal state when death occurs and it merges with the mythic associations of its local group. Additionally (and resembling the north-eastern Arnhem Land concept), the deceased's spirit, or part of it, goes to the Land of the Dead—now located in the sky, but previously known as Braulgwa 'beneath the sea' (cf. Bralgu, the *dua* moiety mythical island of the dead). Mythic beings accompany the spirit on its journey to this Land, but remain attached to their own mythic tracks and local group territories and do not apparently remain at Braulgwa.

The main religious ritual on Groote consists of singing the deceased's spirit to this Land of the Dead. It is in three parts. First, the spirit is taken by its local group kin, through song. The ancestral spirits are brought back from Braulgwa (traditionally, with the spirit of the dead person) on a journey to the deceased's camp; on their arrival, his possessions are destroyed ritually, totemic dances are performed, and close relatives mourn and cut themselves. Second, the ancestral spirits are taken on a journey through their local group territories, along various mythic tracks, and are indeed said to be accompanied by the relevant mythic beings. Third, they are taken to an important place in the deceased's country, where his local group siblings and others in this kin category are painted with totemic designs: this releases them from certain restrictions to which they have been subjected since his death. With this ritual completed, the spirits are returned to the Land of the Dead. About a year after these mortuary rites, a lock of hair is 'sung into' a dillybag, to be kept for a number of years by the deceased's kin in remembrance of him. It is finally taken to the deceased's territory to be buried or stored away. Songs accompany this, and these concern the tracks of various mythic beings.

A delayed mortuary rite is held on the death of an important ritual leader. This is called Babara or Amunduraria, and is essentially a remembrance ritual. The songs and dances are built round the travels of the 'culture hero' Blaur, who is said to have journeyed from Groote to the mainland. Women participate in the opening and closing stages of the ritual, but have no specialized role to play; all other parts are secret-sacred, and these include totemic dances and the use of sacred objects. Finally, a brief rite is carried out to free a person who has been 'placed' on an important site associated with Blaur. The rite consists of singing along Blaur's track until the site is reached (in the song cycle), when the person who has been so 'placed' and has been consequently declared *anggwabugwaba* (tabu) is now painted and declared 'free' or normalized (that is, no longer in direct contact with the supernatural).

The mortuary rituals of Bathurst and Melville Islands have attracted much attention for their use of elaborate posts which are placed on and around the grave. Spencer (1914: 228-39) described the rites and the objects used in them; Mountford (1958: 60-121) has provided more detailed information, and so have Hart and Pilling (1960: 90-3), Goodale (1959a: 3-13) and more recently M. Brandl. Mountford calls the rituals Pukamuni. However, this term, variously spelt (*pukumani, pukamani, pukimani* or *bugamani*), has also a less restricted meaning: it refers to a condition or state of being tabu. In fact, this concept is one of the most significant keys to an understanding of Tiwi culture. The mourners are *pukumani* for the whole period of the mortuary rites. The condition and the label of *pukumani* apply also to novices in the *kulama* (see under ii. *Initiation*), women in childbirth, corpses until buried, grave posts, and so on (see Hart and Pilling 1960: 88-9).

The body of a dead Tiwi is buried and some of his (or her) personal possessions are placed nearby. The spirit of a dead person (*mopaditi*) is dangerous, but remains near the grave 'until the time comes for [it] to leave the locality' (Mountford 1958: 64). His canoe is specially treated after the first *pukumani* rite, to remove his *mopaditi*: if this were not done, the *mopaditi* would warn sea creatures and spoil fishing. A dead woman's *mopaditi* is dangerous to her husband, and his body odour must be masked or disguised if he is not to attract her. Most of the rites emphasize the dangerous qualities of the deceased's spirit, although other themes come into them too; for example, some of the songs and dances recall incidents in the life of the deceased. (For a discussion of such mourning songs, see C. Berndt 1950b: 286-332, especially 289-305.)

Two months after the actual burial, preliminary ceremonies begin. By that time, all the ceremonial tasks allocated by the chief mourners have been accomplished. (Hart and Pilling [*ibid.*] stress the complex network of obligations, debts and credits which is built up in this way, the major activity being the making of the grave posts.) A series of *ilania* dances and songs reflects the relations between the mourners (who are *pukumani*) and 'workers'. In one sequence, workers return from the grave site where they have been cutting posts and a ceremonial fight takes place: in another the people who are *pukumani* fill baskets with food for the workers. There is also a wide range of 'totemic' dances. Finally, all of the participants are decorated, some with ornate facial designs. Mountford (1958: 81-91) divides the rites into five phases: the 'opening' dances in which grief is expressed and events in the life of the deceased are re-enacted; further dances and songs follow, many focusing on the deceased; the payment of the workers; the erecting of the posts at the grave; and, lastly, when the posts are in place, the bushes covering the grave are removed and men and women throw themselves wailing on top of one another at the base of the posts. Traditionally, the beards of chief mourners are now plucked, the painted decorations are washed from their bodies, and they are released form their *pukumani* state. Mountford (*ibid.*: 120) notes that at least one of the posts placed on a grave represents a human being: the *mopaditi* is said to think this is its own son or one of its old companions, and to remain there talking to it.

Generally, the rites are designed to propitiate the deceased and to control the dangerous *mopaditi*. While these intentions are explicit and ritual is believed to keep the spirit from its relatives, what happens after that is not so clear. Hart and Pilling (1960: 9) speak of the

Australian mainland as Tibambinumi, the home of the dead 'to which all Tiwi souls went after death'. Mountford (*ibid.*: 61) also says there is a spirit land—'the *mopaditi*s are eternal'. M. Brandl reports that by 1969 no such land of the dead was acknowledged. Mountford (*ibid.* 61) refers to the *mopaditi* of an infant, who some months after death becomes a *budabuda*, a spirit child, re-entering its mother. Adult *mopaditi* return to their own totemic places, the localities in which they had been born as human beings. The relationship between them and the *pitapitui*, the ordinary spirit children, is not clear. But just as the mythic being Purukupali was associated with the *pitapitui*, so too he is credited with responsibility for the first Tiwi mortuary rituals.

The tribes of the Daly River practised various forms of body-disposal after a death: but usually they burned the deceased's belongings, collected the ashes and buried them near the remains. Traditionally, delayed mortuary rites extended intermittently over several years. At the final ritual, food and gifts were placed on the grave or at the exposure-platform, and a feast was held when 'the dead person is finally ushered out of the world of the living' (Stanner 1933: 26). Stanner emphasizes that there is (was) a general belief in immortality: the soul (*mir*) survives death and enters a new form of existence in a land of the dead (called by Ngulugwonga, Anmel): it becomes, or part of it becomes, a *barung*, a spirit of the dead, and can harm the living. The *mir* (see under i. *Birth*), the agent of a spirit child, itself has mythic associations with the Dreaming.

Stanner (1959-61: 90-7) analyses Murinbata mortuary rites. In the last of six phases, spread over a number of years, 'men of many clans and both moieties gathered in large numbers to bury a man's ashes within his clan-estate': the ashes are pressed into his ancestral soil by dancing feet. And, the mortuary cycle 'was really a co-operative effort by the living to help a human spirit [her *ngjapan*] make the transition from the here-and-now to after-life' (*ibid.*: 91). Stanner speaks of freeing the spirit and destroying the deceased's social identity, even to stamping its ashes into the earth, symbolizing that the soul was separated from what had been its earthly manifestation through a 'totem' agent at birth: 'the spirit of the dead sat or perched upon [the bier] "to look after his own bones", until his remains were pounded into the earth at the *mulunu* rite'. In this way, the spirit of the dead was 'freed to make a new entry into the cycle of life' (*ibid.*: 103, Table I, H)—although on a following page (*ibid.*: 107) Stanner says the spirit of the dead is permitted 'to seek a new, positive locus and status of life on a new plane different from but connected with the old'. However, the evidence makes it plain that the soul or spirit, as something which has come out of the Dreaming (as an agent or otherwise), assumes in life a personal identity which is lost on death, although it supposedly re-enters the Dreaming. There are two contrary views, not necessarily incompatible. One has it that the soul, after the death of its body, enters a land of the dead; the other, that the soul watches its earthly remains being danced into the ground. This last could be interpreted, not so much in terms of a loss of socio-personal identity, but as symbolizing its return in part to its own country. Falkenberg (1962: 251), also speaking of the Murinbata, notes that the deceased's spirit 'will always return to its own spirit home, even though the person dies far away from home'. While the data are unclear, the inference which can be drawn is probably that rebirth is indicated: first as a *wakal* (child: *ngarit'ngarit* and *kura'manganat*; see under i. *Birth*), then as a *ngjapan* (deceased's spirit) and a return to a *wakal*; or symbolized as 'times of plenty' (*wakal*: abundance of natural species) and 'times of scarcity' (*ngjapan*: *ibid.*: 251), in cyclical terms. At the same time, although among the Murinbata there are two kinds of *ngjapan* (depending on their *ngarit'ngarit* and *kura'manganat* manifestations), these *ngjapan* 'of each local clan are invisible supporters of the members of the clan ...' (*ibid.*: 241).

The Walbiri (Meggitt 1962: 317-30) avoid 'the deceased's matrispirit in mobile form'. A dying man's 'conception' Dreaming is painted on his back, and men of his matriline rub their chests against him and seek a clue to the identity of his 'murderer' (where the man's death has been attributed to sorcery): further actions are designed to induce the matrispirit to leave the camp and its relatives. When the deceased's shelter and its contents are burnt, this too is an attempt to drive away the ghost. Later, the corpse is put on a tree platform: in the case of a man, the head points to his 'lodge'-Dreaming country; a woman's head points to her conception-Dreaming country—'in order to facilitate the return of the spirit', which emerges via the corpse's mouth. One interesting feature is the painting of the deceased's conception-Dreaming on the back of each sister of a widow or widower. The matrispirit of the deceased is also believed to help a native doctor in conducting an inquest in search of a victim's 'murderer'. Final disposal occurs about a year or so afterward, when the skeletal remains (except for the armbones) are smashed up and put in a termite mound, the site being left unmarked.

Meggitt (*ibid.*: 317) speaks of the destruction at death of an individual's personality, which disintegrates into its basic components; 'the conception- and lodge-totems return to their spirit-homes, while the matrispirit soon dissipates completely'. It is the patrispirit (*bilirba*) which returns to its own country. The conception spirit is also tied to the land and it too is said to return there—but the *guruwari* intermediary (the matrispirit: see i. *Birth*) does not; instead, it 'becomes a person's ghost, *manbaraba*' (*ibid.*: 207-8). Munn (1970: 142) says that *guruwari* has two primary meanings, one referring to ancestral emblemic designs, the other to the 'invisible fertility powers or essence of the ancestor which, like his visible marks, he leaves in the country'. Beliefs about the partition (so to speak) of a person's spirit at death are quite common; but in this instance, in spite of the fortuitous nature of the *guruwari* relationship, there seems to be a direct linkage between the *guruwari* and re-birth, even though this is framed generally and its personal-indicator is no longer relevant. It underlines the belief that a person as a person is not immortal, but as part of the Dreaming he is not entirely lost and is indeed eligible for re-emergence.

Kaberry (1935: 34-47) discusses mourning ritual at Forrest River. The aim in much of this is to discover the 'murderer' (by sorcery) of the deceased. However, she also notes the vagueness of beliefs about spirits of the dead. Some hold that they become shooting stars: others, that they are taken by spirits to Niligu, the Land of the Dead. Others again emphasize that the *djuari* (spirit) stays by its former body and, if it was a married man, follows its widow. In the Kular and Lyne River areas, young children who die are said to return to their spirit centres to await re-birth—not necessarily through the same mothers.

The deferred mortuary rites, says Kaberry, are 'one of the most spectacular features of tribal life': they are focused on a bundle of the deceased's bones which have been collected and prepared. The rites involve conventionalized conflict between incoming visitors (who have been sent the bones for special treatment) and the locals (the bereaved) as one means of resolving sorcery accusations. Gifts are made to those who have kept the bones, and in exchange the bundle is handed over to the mourners—the bones are thus returned to the deceased's own country. Among the Bugai of north Forrest River (Kaberry 1936: 396), the deceased's bones 'are taken back to his spirit-centre and hidden in a cave near the pool'. In another context (Kaberry 1935: 46), the bones are divided, and what happens to them depends on the tribe concerned. For example, a bundle is returned to the deceased's spirit home (where he was originally found as a spirit child by his father), or buried by a mother where she originally hid her deceased son's umbilical cord, or placed by a mother's brother where the deceased was initiated. Also, pictures of *djuari* are painted on rock shelters in memory of the dead. Kaberry (1939: 209-18) refers to a small piece of bone or a lock of hair being kept: this enables a *djuari* to warn the wearer of impending danger, to teach new song-dances, or to instruct a native doctor. 'Some of the *djuari*' she says, 'are reincarnated in the living: others continue to wander over the land and are a source of protection to their kindred': this should read, more correctly, 'some part of the *djuari*', rather than 'some of'. Also, with reference to the Forrest River groups (*ibid.*: 44-5), the spirit of a dead person may follow a female mourner or transfer its attentions to another who receives food from her, and in this way enter her and be re-born as her child.

Among the Gugadja-Mandjildjara and the Walmadjeri of the Western Desert, now in the Balgo area of the southern Kimberleys, disposal of the dead and beliefs surrounding the deceased's spirit fall within the delayed-mortuary ritual-*djuari* complex, and in general resemble the Walbiri patterning. However, the emphasis is on the identification of the *djugur* Dreaming (referring to the local descent group) and the *djarin* (the 'conception totem'). Further, although the deceased's spirit is divisible, a major part of it does not lose its individual identity because that identity is believed to be eternal: the dead *and* the living are identified within the Dreaming, and in mytho-ritual songs.

Lommel (1952: 37-9) discusses death among the Unambal; and Petri (1968: 277-87) has a general coverage on 'Becoming and Passing Away', including beliefs about the soul and about the 'other world'. See also Elkin (1938/64: Chapter XIII) and R. and C. Berndt (1964/68: Chapter XIII).

Kaberry's comment on the disposal of bone-bundles provides, in effect, a summarized statement which links death with the land, with birth and with initiation. The general evidence demonstrates this kind of association, which is symbolized in a variety of ways.

Coming into being, as an ordinary person, entails admission that there are forces which lie outside the *immediate* control of man, and without which life cannot exist or continue. Beliefs cluster round the entry of a foetus-animator which provides a meaning to existence: it is not simply a matter of chance, but part of an overall plan or design.

Ritual action is designed to ensure that the essentially unpredictable becomes, in the process, predictable: that it is brought under control, and that it is humanized. In regard to human birth, the element of predictability is more obvious. At one level, ritual is not specifically needed to ensure the entry of a spirit child into its human vehicle—even though religious ritual does, more often than not, emphasize a fertility theme. In individual cases, this aspect is taken for granted—that spirit children do come from the Dreaming and do serve as animators. Transference usually takes place through a mundane act, even though that act itself is designated a special or unusual act. In most cases, a spirit child requires no ritual inducement to enter its human vehicle.

At another level, its Dreaming origin is often significant, and the two extremes are the *guruwari* on one hand and the *djugur-djarin* on the other. A spirit child's position in the Dreaming (through whatever channel it comes) has some relevance to its potential position *vis-à-vis* human religious activity and membership in a specific socio-ritual group. Entry into the ordinary world of Aboriginal man does not diminish its essential sacredness.

Death and birth are two sides of the one coin. Conceptually they bear a close similarity. Given the assumption that at birth no ritual is needed, initiation can be thought of, not as a 'ritual death' but as a delayed birth ritual—as being concerned with 'the real social emergence'. Ritual is most obviously relevant in that context, because from that point onward the serious business of living begins. This parallels mortuary ritual. It is not so much at an actual death that ritual is significant. (Of course, ritual acts do accompany a death, but they are mostly of a minor nature.) Mortuary ritual really commences with the delayed rites that follow some time after a death and continue over a fairly long period. These too can be identified as being a form of initiation or transformation.

Looking at it in this light, we come closer to an understanding of Aboriginal belief in this respect. Birth and death are not seen as polar opposites but as parallel experiences, which call for consideration of man's spirit or soul and pose the problem of man's existence as a person and as a social being. The *first* initiation (as noted above, under ii. *Initiation*) is a ritual induction into the Dreaming—the recognition that man's spirit is sacred, and that this quality must be preserved and enhanced. It is also an attempt to use, constructively, the power inherent in man's spirit because of its connection, in one form or another, with the mythic beings. The *second* initiation is a 'birth in reverse', without a human agent (that is, a mother), through which a spirit is released from its immediate human responsibilities so that it may return to the sacred world of the Dreaming. In this way, it is not lost to man. What has been taken from the Dreaming is returned to it: and what returns to it, is confidently expected to come back to man.

This Chapter (Four) is continued in the next Fascicle.

Full bibliography for Chapter Four is to be found at the end of that Chapter, in Fascicle Three.

ILLUSTRATIONS

Preamble

This Fascicle includes two chapters, the second continuing into Fascicle Three. The first relates to north-eastern Australia (Chapter Three). Since I have not carried out research in this region, I have had to rely on the photographs supplied from elsewhere. Of particular importance are those from Cape York: here we have examples from Aurukun, on the western side of that peninsula. As far as the masked dancers are concerned, unfortunately, only one example is available.

Passing from Chapter Three we come to North Australia, which includes Arnhem Land—an area rich in accessible pictorial material. Most of the illustrations provided here are contemporary, and in this Fascicle are focused on mortuary ritual and initiation. Photographic coverage for the Fertility cults appears in Fascicle Three. As in the last Fascicle, emphasis is placed on iconography in its social context, and in relation to the Aborigines themselves.

Acknowledgements

Grateful acknowledgement is made to the various persons who assisted with illustrations. Mr. F. D. McCarthy, then Principal of the Australian Institute of Aboriginal Studies, kindly supplied a selection of photographs from his Aurukun research (that is, Figures 1 to 11). Figure 12 was obtained from the Adelaide *Advertiser*, through the Melbourne *Herald*: it was originally taken by the late Professor D. F. Thomson of the University of Melbourne in 1928-29. Figures 13 to 18 are from Dr. Maria Brandl, formerly a postgraduate research student in the Department of Anthropology, University of Western Australia, with a grant from the Australian Institute of Aboriginal Studies. Figures 19 and 47 to 51 are from Dr. David Turner, formerly a postgraduate research student in the Department of Anthropology, University of Western Australia, with a grant from the Australian Institute of Aboriginal Studies: now in the Department of Sociology, Australian National University. Figures 27 and 28 are from the Rev. H. Shepherdson of Elcho Island, and were obtained from him in 1947. Figures 41 to 46 are illustrated by the kind permission of Mr. R. Thorne of Elcho Island, who took the photographs at Yirrkalla, north-eastern Arnhem Land. Figures 54 to 62 are reproduced with the kind permission of Dr. Maria Brandl, who carried our fieldwork in the Melville and Bathurst Islands area in 1969.

Some of the figures illustrated here have been published previously in various other works. The following comments provide some indication of this. Figures 1, 2 and 10 appear in F. D. McCarthy's 'The Dancers of Aurukun', *Australian Natural History*, March 1964, pages 296-300, as does a variant of the one illustrated in Figure 7; Figure 12 appears in D. F. Thomson, 'The Hero Cult, Initiation and Totemism on Cape York', *Journal of the Royal Anthropological Institute*, Vol. LXIII, 1933; Figure 20 in R. Berndt, *Kunapipi*, Melbourne, 1951. Similar photographs to that illustrated in Figure 33 have been reproduced in R. M. and C. H. Berndt, *Sexual Behaviour in Western Arnhem Land*, Viking Fund Publications in Anthropology, No. 16, 1951, and in R. M. and C. H. Berndt, *The First Australians*, Sydney, 1952/69. Figure 34 also appears in the latter volume, as does a similar one illustrated in Figure 63.

DESCRIPTION OF PLATES

Figures 1 to 11 constitute the Aurukun series, involving an annual ceremony or series of rites. These performances are linked to totem centres (see this Fascicle, Chapter Three, 2), and refer to the increase of the natural species, etc. associated with them. They closely resemble the Wik-Munkan rituals discussed in the main text of this Fascicle. Many of them include wooden sculptures of the 'totemic' creatures, some naturalistic in representation and life-sized; the human figures are approximately up to four feet in height. McCarthy (*ibid.*) notes that such sculptures were not made in pre-European times. However, we do have the example of Arnhem Land, where simple, conventionalized figures were traditional; while even if such work was uncommon or rare in the Aurukun area, traditionally symbolic posts or brush bundles would probably have been made for this purpose.

Figure 1. This depicts an enactment relating to Crow (*atha*) and Gecko Lizard (*pantj*) at Aneiyam on the Archer River, where an ancestral spirit man named Sara created the spirit centre of the *kerindun* clan. There the Crow and the Lizard established their *auwa* centre. In the illustration are four carved figures: the Crow, two Lizards and two Doves (*kolbata*). The three principal dancers wear headbands and carry 'wands' decorated with white cockatoo feathers: behind is a row of men clapping to the singing.
    Photo: F. D. McCarthy, 1963.

Figure 2. This concerns the taipan snake and pelicans and illustrates part of the myth relating to the abduction of Blue Tongue Lizard's wife by the Taipan man. The two principal actors represent a man and his wife who 'turn into 'snakes: they squat at each side of the figure of Blue Tongue Lizard's wife. The two men holding sticks are pelicans. In the foreground is a sculptured representation of the taipan. In a subsequent fight (not shown here), Taipan was bitten into two parts by the Blue Tongue Lizard man. In the background are onlookers.
    Photo: F. D. McCarthy, 1963.

Figure 3. This concerns the ritual performance of a ghost (*ornya*) looking for the Whale man (*akum*), with whom he eventually dances. Ornya was a man before becoming a ghost, and is associated with the Whale's *auwa* centre at Pundata on the Love River. In this figure, the carved whale is lying on the ground (central). Presumably, the actor holding the whale is Ornya. There is no explanation of the men holding spears. In the background are onlookers clapping and singing.
    Photo: F. D. McCarthy, 1963.

Figure 4. This illustrates the barramundi (*wunkum*) rite, simulating the spearing of that fish—shown as a carved wooden object, between the two main dancers. Barramundi was a man at Aukmunka on the Kirke River where, as he was speared, he went down into his *auwa* centre. In the background are the onlookers, singing.

Photo: F. D. McCarthy, 1963.

Figure 5. This illustrates the ritual of the salt water crocodile (*pikowa*) and the fresh water crocodile (*kena*). Two carved wooden crocodiles face each other and the two performers represent them in human form as they quarrel. In the Dreaming, Pikowa abducted and married women normally in an avoidance relationship to him. However, he refused to give Kena a wife, and as a result Kena killed Pikowa in a spear fight. Pikowa 'turned into' a crocodile and his wives into various fish at a place called Itta. In the background are onlookers and singers.

Photo: F. D. McCarthy, 1963.

Figure 6. This ritual dance represents the harpooning of the *jiboom* fish (left) and the *jarapanek* dolphin (right), with a background of singers and onlookers.

Photo: F. D. McCarthy, 1963.

Figure 7. This illustrates a mythical fight between Muipaka, a spirit being, and a Plover (*tultul*): Tultul abducted Muipaka's wife, and was eventually killed by Muipaka. In the Figure, the upright poles represent two other plover men who tried to help the first in his fight with Muipaka. Between them lies an object representing the shield with which Muipaka struck Tultul on the neck, killing him. The two rows of dancing men are plovers holding their dancing 'wands'. Muipaka is not shown, but in another scene is depicted as a wooden figure with right arm raised.

Photo: F. D. McCarthy, 1963.

Figure 8. This concerns a fresh water shark (*ningkushin*) who, out hunting, saw an *orpul* (translated by McCarthy as a 'fairy') girl sitting on a rock in a lagoon at Tapundji, near the Kendall River. He wanted to capture her and make her his wife. He prepared himself by smearing clay all over his body to detract from its odour, and holding a branch to hide behind he crept up near to where she was sitting. He speared her, but as he did so she took him down into the water with her, and together they made the *auwa* centre of this shark. The Figure illustrates a wooden model of the shark and the *orpul*. The onlookers are clapping as they sing the relevant songs.

Photo: F. D. McCarthy, 1963.

Figure 9. This relates to the wallaby (*punka*). Men track the wallaby, imitating its hopping. In the illustration, three wallaby men struggle with the wooden model, indicating a fight between these animals, after which they spread over the countryside. Onlookers clap as they sing.

Photo: F. D. McCarthy, 1963.

Figure 10. This represents the curlew (*pipapepe*) dance. Participants imitate the posture and cry of this bird. This symbolizes an ancestral man who went into an *auwa* centre at Kutun, turning into a curlew as he did so. Behind them are the singers and onlookers.

Photo: F. D. McCarthy, 1963.

Figure 11. This scene also concerns the taipan snake (see Figure 2). In this case it is his son who has abducted the wife of Blue Tongue Lizard. He, too, was bitten in half by the husband during a fight. In the illustration is Taipan's head 'half' upright on the ground. As he died, he 'turned into' Tu Apletj, who taught the taipan men (local 'totemic' group: the row of four dancers, holding poles) to perform the dance shown here.

Photo: F. D. McCarthy, 1963.

Figure 12. This illustration depicts the *ngartji kintja* (tabu or secret-sacred ground) at Stewart River (Yintjingga tribe), on Princess Charlotte Bay, eastern side of Cape York Peninsula. Masked dancers (*ompoibo*) dance across the ground toward a group of men with novices. The *ompoibo* figures wear headdresses of four sticks ornamented with feathers and are completely covered with the *watu*, the ceremonial dress of the *okainta* (initiation) ritual. These dances relate to the mythic being I'wai (see this Fascicle, Chapter Three, 2).

Photo: D. F. Thomson 1928-29.

Figures 13 to 18 concern the *kulama* rituals of the Tiwi of Bathurst and Melville Islands. See this Fascicle, Chapter Four, ii. The illustrations here were taken in 1969 at Snake Bay and Garden Point on Melville Island.

Figure 13. This shows an elderly *kulama* participant sprinkling red-ochre on the mound which encircles the *kulama* ground. In the foreground is the *kulama* fire, containing pieces of ant-bed (termite mound) to maintain heat. Under the paperbark (to the right of the fire), propped up by a digging stick, is a basket of yams.

Photo: Maria Brandl, Snake Bay, 1969.

Figure 14. This depicts the *kulama* ring place with its central fire for cooking yams (see Figure 13). Participants wait for the fire to burn low, when the yams will be placed in the oven. On the right, a man fashions a grass wreath to be placed over the yams as they cook.

Photo: Maria Brandl, Snake Bay, 1969.

Figure 15. This shows participants carefully peeling the yams after their removal from the oven. Later they will be sliced and rubbed over their bodies. The yams rest on sheets of paperbark, and to the lower left is the oven itself with cooked yams surrounded by the grass wreath (see Figure 14).

Photo: Maria Brandl, Snake Bay, 1969.

Figure 16. This illustrates participants anointing or rubbing themselves with the cooked yams. The man on the left places yams on his wife's head: the one on the right, on the head of a classificatory cross-cousin.

Photo: Maria Brandl, Snake Bay, 1969.

Figure 17. This depicts singing poses in the *kulama* ritual: beside the man is his wife, who echoes his words as he beats time. His clapping sticks are shown: one he holds; the other, resting on the blanket, is of a fish design.

Photo: Maria Brandl, Garden Point, 1969.

Figure 18. This shows a typical singing pose in the *kulama*. The singer holds clapping-sticks, and beside him is the dismantled oven. The peeled and sliced yams are in the billy-can, soaking in water.

Photo: Maria Brandl, Snake Bay, 1969.

Figure 19. Aboriginal women bring novices covered with blankets to the men for circumcisional rites. At Angurugu mission station, Groote Eylandt.

Photo: D. Turner, Groote Eylandt, 1969.

Figure 20. This illustration is a reproduction of a drawing, done with lumber crayons on brown paper, depicting part of the Wawalag myth (see illustrations to Fascicle One; also this Fascicle, Chapter Four, ii and Fascicle Three, Chapter Four continued, under Fertility Rites). The artists are Mawulan and his son, Wondjug, Riradjingu dialect unit, Yirrkalla, north-eastern Arnhem Land.

Briefly, the drawing (right hand panel) shows in the top left hand corner the elder and younger Wawalag sisters, with the former's child inside their shade. In the right hand bottom corner are the sacred waters of Muruwul (Miraraminar) in which Yulunggul lives with other Lightning Snakes (pythons): one of these snakes is shown on the left side of the waters: and around this whole area grow *gulwiri* 'cabbage' palms (represented by trunks and v-like branches). The zigzag design diagonally across the drawing is the track from the Wawalag's shade to Muruwul; the round circles are stones that were cast aside. It is along this track that the elder sister's afterbirth blood flows and attracts the snake. Yulunggul's head is also shown (top right).

In the left hand panel, the central right circle is the Wawalag's shade (the small child is inside, but not clearly visible in this illustration), with tracks leading toward it. The Two Sisters dance around it, in an attempt to keep Yulunggul away. Two large Yulunggul snakes are drawn horizontally, and below them a female Yulunggul; between them is the mark left on the ground when the Yulunggul, after swallowing the Wawalag, tried to stand erect but fell over; this forms the shape of the secret-sacred ritual ground. Eventually, Yulunggul vomits the Wawalag near an anthill (top left circle): radiating lines are streams of ants who bite the Wawalag and revive them. Two *gungalung* gecko lizards are shown: they emerge at the beginning of the rainy season. Collected by R. Berndt, Yirrkalla, 1946-47.

> *Figures 21 to 25* comprise secret-sacred sections of the *djunggawon* circumcisional ritual from which novices are excluded, prior to the sequences in the main camp. See this Fascicle, Chapter Four, ii. They show the bringing out of the Wawalag post from the secret place at which it was made: eventually it will be erected in the main camp and will watch over the rituals. This post is sacred, and represents the elder Wawalag sister: she is decorated, and parrakeet feathered tassels hang from her 'head'.

Figure 21. This depicts a man who has uncovered the Wawalag post on the secret-sacred ground: alongside the post, the long pole-like object is the Yulunggul trumpet (or didjeridu); this is later played over prostrate novices who are swallowed as were the Wawalag sisters.

Photo: R. M. Berndt, Yirrkalla, 1946-47.

Figure 22. The Wawalag post commences its journey, symbolic of the Wawalag sisters' travels to the sacred waterhole. The men are singing the relevant sections of the great cycle, and beginning to dance. The man on the left has his sacred dillybag slung across his chest.

Photo: R. M. Berndt, Yirrkalla, 1946-47.

Figure 23. Postulants surround the Wawalag post, calling invocations to the Wawalag.
Photo: R. M. Berndt, Yirrkalla, 1946-47.

Figure 24. Men sing, while others posture as the Wawalag post is moved backward and forward, symbolizing the movements of the elder Wawalag along the track leading to Muruwul.

Photo: R. M. Berndt, Yirrkalla, 1946-46.

Figure 25. Men cluster around the Wawalag post, calling invocations, while the songman claps his sticks; this concludes part of the travels of the elder sister. In the background is the cleared space of the secret-sacred ground.

Photo: R. M. Berndt, Yirrkalla, 1946-47.

Figure 26. Four *djunggawon* circumcisional novices painted with the sacred emblemic patterns of their dialect units, each referring to their mythic background.

Photo: R. M. Berndt, Yirrkalla, 1946-47.

Figure 27. Djunggawon circumcisional novices on the secret-sacred ground being shown a ritual sequence from the Wawalag myth. A group of men and the novices, decorated with emblemic patterns, stand at the end of the ground, while before them an actor postures clenching a sacred bag between his teeth: before him is another actor decorated in feather-down. At Milingimbi, north-central Arnhem Land, in the late 1930's.

Photo: H. Shepherdson.

Figure 28. This depicts one of a series of 'totemic' rites in the Wawalag cycle performed in the *djunggawon* circumcisional sequence on the secret-sacred ground. The two actors, decorated with feather-down, represent creatures collected by the Two Sisters for food, which instead dived into the sacred waters to join Yulunggul. The two novices are held by their guardians and bear their sacred patterns: the singing man with clapping-sticks stands between them. At Milingimbi, north-central Arnhem Land, in the late 1930's.

Photo: H. Shepherdson.

Figure 29. Watching the non-secret (sacred) section of a *djunggawon* circumcisional ritual in the main camp at Yirrkalla, north-eastern Arnhem Land.

Photo: R. M. Berndt, 1946-47.

Figure 30. This depicts a young novice awaiting circumcision with his guardian resting on a spear. The novice has a headband of wool with tassels typical of *jiridja* moiety decorations, he wears arm bands, and has a sacred pattern painted on his chest: by this stage in the proceedings, the pattern has become blurred.

Photo: R. M. Berndt, Elcho Island, 1966.

Figure 31. Ritual performers in the *ubar* ritual of western Arnhem Land, representing rock wallabies. These mythic beings were responsible for helping Gandagi (kangaroo) to take over the *ubar* from the women. See illustrations of *ubar* sequence in Fascicle One and in this Fascicle, Chapter Four, ii.

Photo: R. M. Berndt, Oenpelli, 1947.

Figure 32. Individual dancing on the *ubar* ground: one man after another dances, each in turn indicating who is to follow by touching him. This is said to be the original dancing first performed by the men when they took over the *ubar* from the women. In the background is the sacred hut or shade, *wangaridja*.

Photo: R. M. Berndt, Oenpelli, 1947.

Figure 33. An *ubar* ritual performance by two men representing *wiliwili* birds. They wear white cockatoo feathers in their hair. See the illustration of a bark painting in Fascicle One, Figure 26, where two actors appear in a similar posture but symbolize different birds.

Photo: R. M. Berndt, Oenpelli, 1947.

Figure 34. Two *wiliwili* bird actors on a pandanus palm, in the concluding ritual of the *ubar*. Around them men clap sticks and sing, calling invocations to the Creative Mother. Women dance round them.

Photo: R. M. Berndt, Oenpelli, 1950.

Figures 35 to 39 illustrate a delayed mortuary ritual. The scenes here took place after the collection of the deceased's bones. See Fascicle One, Figure 11 and this Fascicle, Chapter Four, iii. The bones are placed in a tall hollow-log receptacle which has been carved and decorated with the emblemic patterning of his dialect group, referring to the myths associated with him. This is a *nganuku laragidj*, and represents a mythic or totemic creature: at its head (top), eyes and mouth are depicted—and the deceased's bones are symbolically put back into the creature, back into the Dreaming.

Figure 35. This shows an upright *laragidj* of the *dua* moiety. A group of men sit before it singing; the principal songman and director, second on the left, is undecorated. Dancing men move toward the *laragidj*. The songs concern Bralgu, the *dua* moiety Land of the Dead.

Photo: R. M. Berndt, Yirrkalla, 1946-47.

Figure 36. Dancing before the *dua* moiety *laragidj*: the songman sits in the foreground with his clapping-sticks. Two groups of participants are visible.

Photo: R. M. Berndt, Yirrkalla, 1946-47.

Figure 37. This depicts participants, dancers and singers, and the two *laragidj*: of the *dua* moiety on the left, the *jiridja* moiety on the right.

Photo: R. M. Berndt, Yirrkalla, 1946-47.

Figure 38. A row of dancers move round the *jiridja* moiety *laragidj*. They represent spirits (*mogwoi*) at the *jiridja* Land of the Dead testing the deceased's spirit; all carry spears.

Photo: R. M. Berndt, Yirrkalla, 1946-47.

Figure 39. Before the *jiridja* moiety *laragidj*, symbolically spearing the dead person's spirit. In the foreground, at each side, are men using clapping-sticks and singing.

Photo: R. M. Berndt, Yirrkalla, 1946-47.

Figure 40. Preparing the *jiridja* moiety mast, which will later be erected during a delayed mortuary ritual to farewell the deceased's spirit on its journey to the Land of the Dead.

Photo: R. M. Berndt, Yirrkalla, 1966.

Figures 41 to 46 continue the sequence shown in Figures 16 to 20 in Fascicle One. These concern the delayed mortuary rites held at Yirrkalla, in north-eastern Arnhem Land, in 1968 for Mawulan, a Riradjingu headman who died in November 1967.

Figure 41. Two lines of dancing participants led by the dead man's son, Wondjug, on the way to the mortuary ground. On the left a row of women is headed by the didjeridu player, his instrument supported on the shoulder of a companion. Dancers represent spirits at the *dua* moiety Land of the Dead.

Photo: R. Thorne, Yirrkalla, 1968.

Figure 42. Arriving at the first section of the dancing ground near the dead man's house. A sacred mound has been prepared, representing his spiritual home Jelangbara, at Port Bradshaw, on the coast south of Yirrkalla, sacred to the Djanggawul (see Fascicle Three, Chapter Four continued, under Fertility Rites). Close to the mound, a man sings as he claps his sticks. Alongside of him (left) is the didjeridu player, blowing the sound into the sacred site. Behind is a row of dancing women and men.

Photo: R. Thorne, Yirrkalla, 1968.

Figure 43. Around the sacred mound of Jelangbara. Sacred *rangga* objects (see Fascicle Three, Chapter Four continued, under Fertility Rites) have been put into the mound. These are the life-giving *ganinjeri*, or yam sticks, carried by the Djanggawul Sisters when they reached the north-eastern Arnhem Land coast after their epic canoe trip from the mythical island of Bralgu: they used them as walking sticks, creating life as they prodded the ground. The *ganinjeri* in the illustration have parrakeet-feathered tassels or pendants tipped with seagull feathers.

Before the three *ganinjeri* is Wondjug, the dead man's son, who calls the sacred invocations associated with Jelangbara and the Djanggawul. On the right a man carries over his shoulder a long bag with interwoven feathers, used for keeping *rangga* objects. The two women, on either side, are painted and wear feathered chaplets with hanging pendants as did the Djanggawul Sisters: other women are behind Wondjug.

Photo: R. Thorne, Yirrkalla, 1968.

Figure 44. This is the sand structure which is a stylized representation of Jelangbara, the sacred site of the Djanggawul. Mounds of sand edging this are the sand hills at this place sacred to the *djanda* goanna, which is especially associated with the Djanggawul: other mounds crossing the main outline represent sections of the country. Poles have been erected, and hung with lengths of sacred feathered string. In the background is a row of women. Dancing men move along the screen of boughs led (on the right) by the didjeridu player; on the left is the songman with his clapping-sticks. The songs refer to the 'outside' (public) version of the Djanggawul cycle.

Photo: R. Thorne, Yirrkalla, 1968.

Figure 45. Participants are ranged along the edge of the sand structure, while invocations are called—concerning the country and the Djanggawul.
Photo: R. Thorne, Yirrkalla, 1968.

Figure 46. The sacred sand structure after the rituals have been completed: it is approximately 50 feet long, and about 10 feet across at the top, tapering at the end. The screen of boughs makes up the background.
Photo: R. Thorne, Yirrkalla, 1968.

Figures 47 to 51 concern a mortuary ritual held on Groote Eylandt. See this Fascicle, Chapter Four, iii.

Figure 47. This depicts a group of men during a pause in their singing. Their singing effects the transference of the deceased's spirit from its physical home to the Land of the Dead. All these men are of the dead person's patri-moiety, the leaders of his own local group.
Photo: D. Turner, Angurugu mission station, Groote Eylandt, 1969.

Figure 48. The dead person's possessions are burnt, symbolizing the severing of physical ties between the living and the dead. In the foreground are members of the deceased's local group singing his 'totemic' songs, while women sit clustered together in the background.
Photo: D. Turner, Angurugu mission station, Groote Eylandt, 1969.

Figure 49. Part of the concluding mortuary rites. Food symbolizing the bodies of ancestral beings awaits distribution to certain kinsfolk of the deceased. Smoke will be 'passed over' this food, removing it from the realm of the sacred and making it available for ordinary consumption.
Photo: D. Turner, Angurugu mission station, Groote Eylandt, 1969.

Figure 50. The sand-mound structure representing a sacred site associated with the mythic being Blaur. Ritual leaders are preparing the enclosure. Later, a girl will be placed within it. The songs relevant to Blaur's Dreaming track are sung until this particular site (symbolized by the structure) is reached, when she is painted with ochre and smoke is 'passed over' her: she is then released from her contact with the supernatural.
Photo: D. Turner, Angurugu mission station, Groote Eylandt, 1969.

Figure 51. Typical mortuary dance at Umbakumba, Groote Eylandt. The dancer holds a bunch of spears and a spearthrower.
Photo: D. Turner, Umbakumba, Groote Eylandt, 1969.

Figure 52. A delayed mortuary ritual. The deceased's belongings are heaped up: some of these will later be burnt and the residue distributed to participants (excluding the immediate kin of the dead person). See this Fascicle, Chapter Four continued, *iii*. A songman with arms outstretched sings part of the mythic cycle relevant to the deceased.
Photo: R. M. Berndt, Adelaide River, Northern Territory, 1945.

Figure 53. Dancing in a delayed mortuary ritual: see above Figure, 52.
Photo: R. M. Berndt, Adelaide River, Northern Territory, 1945.

Figures 54 to 62 concern mortuary rituals held on Bathurst and Melville Islands. Following a death, close relatives of the deceased go into mourning. Behavioural restrictions involved are not lifted until the delayed mortuary rituals are completed, which could be about two years. Until recently, the beautifully decorated funerary posts were always erected about the grave. (Figures 61-62 show some of these.)

Figure 54. In this case, the dead person was a man. By the open grave, at which the coffin has been placed, one of his classificatory mothers' brothers dances, hands on the belly indicating that relationship. The woman dancing in the background is one of the dead man's classificatory fathers' sisters. Others beat time.
Photo: Maria Brandl, Snake Bay, Melville Island, 1969.

Figure 55. In this case, the dead person was a woman. The coffin has been lowered into the grave. The young man directing the burial is her brother's son's son. Behind, grief-stricken mourners are being restrained. In the background is the government-owned truck which transported the coffin to the burial ground.
Photo: Maria Brandl, Snake Bay, Melville Island, 1969.

Figure 56. Among the graves of 'Christian' Aborigines (see cross over grave), a woman sings a traditional-style song of grief for the woman who has just been buried, her husband's father's sister.
Photo: Maria Brandl, Snake Bay, Melville Island, 1969.

Figure 57. A man has died at Bathurst Island. At Snake Bay on Melville Island, on hearing the news, his sister's daughter (foreground, right) organizes a ritual with the help of her husband. It begins with the lighting of a fire to attract the dead person's spirit.
Photo: Maria Brandl, Snake Bay, Melville Island, 1969.

Figure 58. A man decorates his wife for a mortuary rite to be held later that day. It is for his sister's son, who had recently died.
Photo: Maria Brandl, Snake Bay, Melville Island, 1969.

Figure 59. An old man died at the Bathurst Island mission station, and was buried there. His clothes and suitcase were kept, to be buried later during the ritual depicted here. Alongside the case, one of his widows stands wailing and singing as she beats her clapping-sticks. The case is placed at the edge of the hole in which it will be buried. In the background is a second widow of the deceased, also singing. Others sit awaiting their turn to sing and dance.
Photo: Maria Brandl, Bathurst Island mission station, 1969.

Figure 60. The principal mourner dances in a mortuary ritual, while other performers sing and beat time.
Photo: Maria Brandl, Bathurst Island mission station, 1969.

Figure 61. Painting a mortuary post for a forthcoming ritual. The artist is smoking a crab-claw pipe.
Photo: Maria Brandl, Melville Island, 1969.

Figure 62. Mortuary posts stand outside the deceased's house. The final rituals have been completed, and one pole is wrapped ready for despatch to a purchaser in Darwin.
    Photo: Maria Brandl, Melville Island, 1969.

Figure 63. Observing a *pukumani* tabu, in this case associated with mourning. The man may not touch food, and consequently must be fed by another person as shown here.
    Photo: R. M. Berndt, Bathurst Island, 1947.

PLATES AND MAPS

1. Aurukun ritual: Crow and Gecko Lizard enactment.

2. Aurukun ritual: Taipan Snake and Blue Tongue Lizard's wife. A mythic enactment.

3. Aurukun ritual: Whale man and the *ornya* Ghost. A mythic enactment.

4. Aurukun ritual: barramundi fish rite.

5. Aurukun ritual: salt water and fresh water Crocodiles. A mythic enactment.

6. Aurukun ritual: symbolic harpooning of *jiboom* fish and dolphin.

7. Aurukun ritual: mythic fight between Muipaka and Plover.

8. Aurukun ritual: attempted abduction of an *orpul* (spirit girl) by fresh water Shark.
A mythic enactment.

9. Aurukun ritual: fight between Dreaming Wallaby men.

10. Aurukun ritual: dance of the Dreaming Curlew man (centre).

11. Aurukun ritual: the son of Taipan Snake bitten in half by Blue Tongue Lizard after abducting Blue Tongue's wife. A mythic enactment.

12. Masked dancers before a group of men and novices. Princess Charlotte Bay, Cape York Peninsula.

13. *Kulama* rituals: preparing the *kulama* ground. Melville Island.

14. *Kulama* rituals: oven on *kulama* ground for cooking sacred yams.

15. *Kulama* rituals: peeling sacred yams after removal from oven. Melville Island.

16. *Kulama* rituals: participants anointing themselves with the sacred yams. Melville Island.

17. *Kulama* rituals: *kulama* singing pose: woman echoes her husband's singing. Melville Island.

18. *Kulama* rituals: *kulama* singing pose.

19. Women bring covered novices to the men for circumcision. Groote Eylandt.

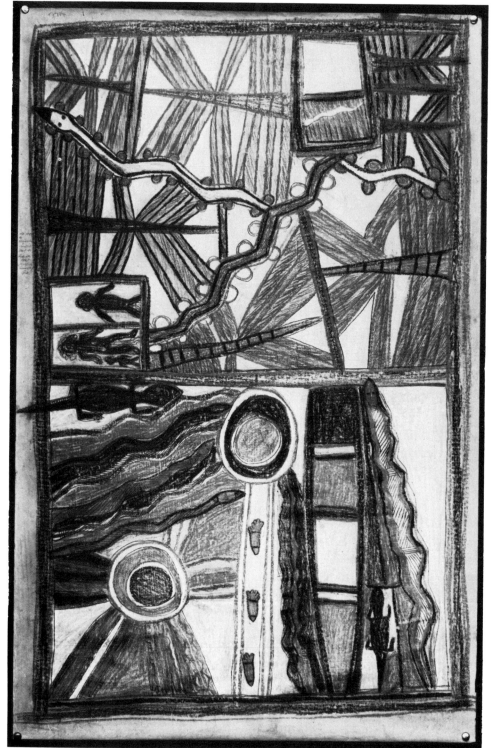

20. Drawing of events at the sacred place of Muruwul in the great Wawalag and Yulunggul myth. Yirrkalla, Arnhem Land.

21. *Djunggawon* ritual: The Wawalag post on the secret-sacred ground, with the Yulunggul trumpet, resting against a tree. Yirrkalla, Arnhem Land.

22. *Djunggawon* ritual. The Wawalag post commences its journey. Yirrkalla, Arnhem Land.

23. *Djunggawon* ritual: calling invocations to the Wawalag. Yirrkalla, Arnhem Land.

24. *Djunggawon* ritual: posturing with Wawalag post. Yirrkalla, Arnhem Land.

25. *Djunggawon* ritual: conclusion of travels of Wawalag post. Yirrkalla, Arnhem Land.

26. *Djunggawon* novices painted with sacred patterns.
Yirrkalla, Arnhem Land.

27. Novices being shown a *djunggawon* ritual sequence on the secret-
sacred ground. Milingimbi, Arnhem Land.

28. 'Totemic' ritual dance in *djunggawon* series on secret-sacred ground. Milingimbi, Arnhem Land.

29. Watching non-secret section of *djunggawon* in main camp at Yirrkalla, Arnhem Land.

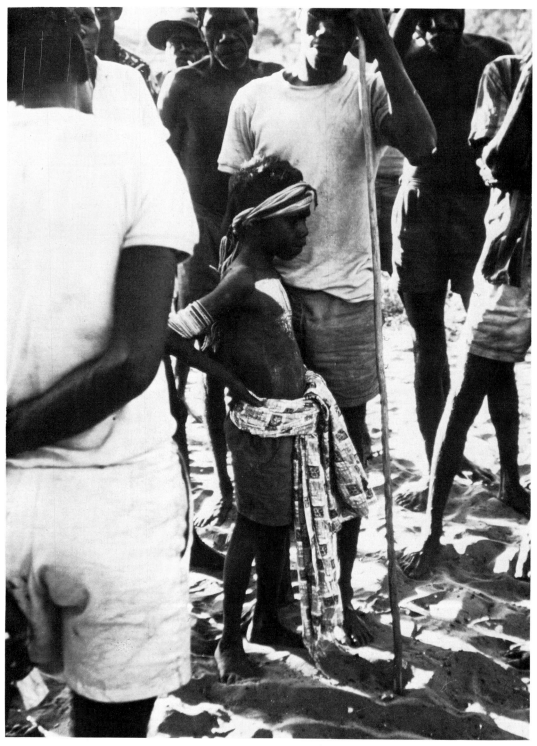

30. A novice awaiting circumcision. Elcho Island, Arnhem Land.

32. Individual dancing on the *ubar* ground. Oenpelli, Arnhem Land.

31. *Ubar* ritual, Arnhem Land. Participants represent rock wallabies. Oenpelli, Arnhem Land.

33. *Ubar* ritual act by two men representing *wiliwili* birds. Oenpelli, Arnhem Land.

34. Concluding rite in the *ubar*. Two *wiliwili* bird actors on pandanus palm, calling invocations.
Oenpelli, Arnhem Land.

35. Delayed mortuary ritual, Yirrkalla. Singing and dancing before *dua* moiety *laragidj* pole.

36. Delayed mortuary ritual, Yirrkalla. Dancing before *dua* moiety *laragidj* pole.

37. Delayed mortuary ritual, Yirrkalla. Dancers and singers before the *dua* and *jiridja* moiety *laradidj* poles.

38. Delayed mortuary ritual, Yirrkalla. Participants representing *mogwoi* spirits move round the *jiridja* moiety *laragidj* pole.

39. Delayed mortuary ritual, Yirrkalla. Symbolically spearing the dead person's spirit before the *jiridja* moiety *laragidj* pole.

40. Delayed mortuary ritual, Yirrkalla
Preparing a *jiridja* moiety mast
to farewell the deceased's spirit.

41. Delayed mortuary rites, Yirrkalla. Lines of dancing participants representing spirits in the *dua* moiety Land of the Dead, led by singing man and didjeridu player.

42. Delayed mortuary rites, Yirrkalla. Sacred mound representing the spiritual home of the dead man. This is the sacred place of the Djanggawul at Jelangbara, Port Bradshaw, Arnhem Land.

43. Delayed mortuary rites, Yirrkalla. Invocations being called over the sacred life-giving *ganinjeri* yam sticks of the Djanggawul, erected upright on the mound.

44. Delayed mortuary rites, Yirrkalla. Sacred mound structure representing Jelangbara, the Djanggawul site, with poles hung with lengths of feathered string.

45. Delayed mortuary rites, Yirrkalla. Invocations being called at one side of the Jelangbara mound structure.

46. Delayed mortuary rites. Yirrkalla. Sacred mound structure after the rites have been completed.

47. Mortuary ritual, Groote Eylandt. A group of men pause in their singing, which is said to transfer the deceased's spirit to the Land of the Dead.

48. Mortuary ritual, Groote Eylandt. Burning the dead person's possessions, symbolizing the severing of physical ties between the living and the dead.

49. Mortuary ritual, Groote Eylandt. Food symbolizing the bodies of ancestral beings awaits distribution.

50. Mortuary ritual, Groote Eylandt. A sand mound structure representing a sacred site associated with the mythic being, Blaur. Ritual leaders prepare the enclosure.

51. Mortuary ritual, Groote Eylandt. A typical mortuary dance.

52. Delayed mortuary ritual, Adelaide River, Northern Territory. The deceased's belongings are heaped up for burning and for distribution.

53. Dancing in delayed mortuary ritual, Adelaide River, Northern Territory.

54. Melville Island mortuary rituals. A classificatory brother of the dead person dances at the graveside.

55. Melville Island mortuary rituals. Mourners at a dead woman's burial.

56. Melville Island mortuary rituals. A woman sings a traditional-style song of grief at the graveside.

57. Melville Island mortuary rituals. Rite of lighting a fire to attract the dead person's spirit.

58. Melville Island mortuary rituals. A man decorates his wife for a mortuary rite.

59. Melville Island mortuary rituals. The possessions of a dead man are to be buried separately.
Alongside the case one of his widows sings a song of grief.

60. Melville Island mortuary rituals. The principal mourner dances.

61. Melville Island mortuary rituals. Painting a mortuary post.

62. Melville Island mortuary rituals. Mortuary posts outside the deceased's house

63. Observing a *pukumani* tabu: the mourner is not permitted to feed himself. Bathurst Island.